MYSTICAL CLASSICS OF THE WORLD

# Tao Te Ching

# Tao Te Ching
## The Classic Book of Integrity and the Way
### LAO TZU

TRANSLATED, ANNOTATED, AND WITH AN AFTERWORD
BY VICTOR H. MAIR

WOODCUTS BY DAN HEITKAMP

INTRODUCTION BY HUSTON SMITH

QUALITY PAPERBACK BOOK CLUB

NEW YORK

FOR DAVE,
who dances with the Tao.

The supreme perfection of actionlessness
He attains through renunciation.

*Naiṣkarmyasiddhiṁ paramāṁ*
*Saṁnyāsenādhigacchati.*

Bhagavad Gītā, XVIII.49.3–4


While you . . .
   Focus your breath until it is supremely soft,
   Can you be like a baby?

*Tai . . .*
   *Chuan ch'i chih jou,*
   *Neng ying-erh hu?*

Tao Te Ching, 54.1, 4–5


What is the use of running when we are not on the right way?

*Was hilft laufen, wenn man nicht auf den rechten Weg ist?*

German proverb

# CONTENTS

# Introduction
## by Huston Smith

Because each volume in this set of Mystical Classics of the World ferrets out distinctive regions of mystical consciousness, taken together they provide a striking overview of its landscape. I intend to use my Introduction to each of the six volumes in the set to bring this out. Individually the books speak for themselves and can be read independently of one another, but to see them collectively as a mosaic that offers an overview of the mystic's world they should be read in the sequence in which I position them in my Introductions. For I try in these Introductions to provide the reader with a map for a journey that doubles back across the vast Eurasian landmass that Marco Polo crossed in the opposite direction seven centuries ago. Setting out from its eastern rim—in China with its *Tao Te Ching*, the book in hand—these books, as introduced, proceed through India via the *Bhagavad-Gita*, Tibet via *The Tibetan Book of the Dead*, the Persian/Arab world with Rumi as guide, and the Palestinian corridor via the Kabbalah to come to rest in Europe's *The Way of a Pilgrim*. Readers who make this pilgrimage with me, stopping at each stage of the journey to visit a local, welcoming sage for a day or two, should be able to proceed on life's way with a better understanding of the higher regions of the human spirit, the role those regions have played in human history, and how readers who are interested in doing so might move into those regions themselves.

I begin with a word about the importance of mysticism as such, and this set as a whole. The reasons for the crisis in which the world now finds itself are located in something deeper than particular ways of organizing political systems and economies. In different ways, both the East and the West are going through a single common crisis whose cause is the spiritual condition of the modern world. That condition is characterized by loss—the loss of metaphysical certainties and of transcendence with its higher horizons. It is strange but ultimately quite logical. As soon as human beings started considering themselves the source of the highest meaning in the world and the measure of everything, meaning began to ebb, and the stature of man to shrink. The world lost its human dimension, and man began to lose control of it.

We have been going through a great skepticism, a spiritual desert that has no parallel in history. We are living in the first skeptical civilization, which, if the situation is not reversed, is in danger of spiraling into cynicism and despair. If the world is to change for the better, it must start with a change in the human understanding of things.

Enter this set of Mystical Classics of the World. The mystical is life's highest register, and with the busy-ness of contemporary life in mind, this Quality Paperback Book Club set makes six of its short representative texts available to perhaps the largest audience for which they have ever been packaged. Collectively its six volumes remind us of things we have forgotten, are missing, and (if we have ears to hear) might recover.

In my ordering of its volumes, the set opens with the *Tao Te Ching*, the presiding expression of not only China's mystical consciousness but of all East Asia's, for Japan's, Korea's, and half of Southeast Asia's cultures derived directly from China. Viewed globally, the distinctive feature of East Asian civilization is its social emphasis. We see this particularly in Confucianism, which is as much an ethic as a religion, but taken as a whole East Asian civilization is more occupied than others with the question of how people, if wisely ruled, can live together in peace and harmony. This colors even its mysticism, which typically is the most otherworldly echelon of a civilization. The *Tao Te Ching* builds this social and moral concern into its very title by placing "integrity" (*te*) at its center. If "political strategy" and "utopian architecture" (see Victor H. Mair's Preface, p. xxi) were its only interest it would not be a mystical text, but that it is heavily concerned with these themes betrays its Chinese signature and stands as a healthy reminder that mysticism need not be otherworldly.

Granted its social and ethical concern, what makes the *Tao Te Ching* at the same time a mystical text is its grounding in the Tao, a reality so transcendent that the authors of this text refer to it as "nonbeing" (p. 8) to distinguish it from the kinds of "beings" we are acquainted with in this world. (There is a striking parallel here to frontier physics, which now positions the fundamental process of Nature outside of space and time, but that is in passing.) When we move beyond acknowledging the transcendent Tao to describing it, we face a paradox. This must not deter us, for the *Tao Te Ching* itself forewarns us that "True words seem contradictory" (p. 54). The immediate paradox is that the text tells us that "The names that can be named are not the eternal name" (p. 59) and that "One who knows does not speak;/One who speaks does not know" (p. 25), while prattling on about the Tao on every page.

INTRODUCTION

Fortunately this particular paradox—unlike others that can dog us the rest of our lives—is easily resolved. In its transcendent, self-contained fullness the Tao is ineffable, but our words can point toward it as fingers point to the moon. The moon remains astronomically beyond our fingertips, but our pointing can still be accurate.

Our "fingers" point accurately to the Tao, the *Tao Te Ching* teaches, when they prompt us to think of it as great and mysterious—as awesomely great and mysterious as our imaginations can carry us. To add some specifics to this, the Tao is, as Plotinus said of his One, "that fountain ever on." It is the mother of all things, for ". . . from non-being/The Way gave birth to unity,/Unity gave birth to duality,/Duality gave birth to trinity,/[and] Trinity gave birth to the myriad creatures" (pp. 8-9)—literally "the ten thousand things," which was the Chinese way of referring to the universe. Born before heaven and earth, the Tao is complete, compassionate, unassuming, and reserved, for "A whirlwind does not last the whole morning,/A downpour does not last the whole day" (p. 89).

Perhaps most importantly, despite its yieldingness and reticence, the Tao is, in the end, irresistible and will have its way. This blend of suppleness and power makes water the *Tao Te Ching*'s favorite analogy for the Tao. Water is patient; it can stagnate and let itself be coated with scum if need be. It is as gentle as the morning's dew. It is non-confrontational, even respectful, in circumventing the rocks in a stream. It makes room for everything that enters its pools. It accommodates by assuming the shape of any vessel it is poured into. And it is humble, seeking always the lowest level. Yet along with—or rather because of—

these adaptive, yielding properties, it is ultimately irresistible; it carves canyons out of stone. And so with us as well, the *Tao Te Ching* argues, or better, counsels, for the Tao does not argue. If we conform our lives to it, allowing its virtues to flow through us as we strictly eschew "the brazenness of a bandit" (p. 22), our actions, too, will succeed within human limits. This sounds absurd to worldly ears, but that is to be expected, for "When the inferior man hears the Way,/he laughs at it loudly./If he did not laugh,/it would not be fit to be the Way" (p. 7).

The key phrase the *Tao Te Ching* uses to characterize the dynamic outworkings of the Tao in human affairs is *wu wei*. Literally that phrase translates as "inaction," but in Taoist context its meaning is "no wasted motion," which stated positively comes to minimum friction and pure effectiveness. Aero- and nautical dynamics provide the obvious analogues here, for the smaller the wake of a craft, the more its power goes into getting it to where it wants to go. I find it historically poetic that among traditional vessels, engineers give the Chinese junk the prize for nautical design. Is it surprising, when its rivals in other parts of the world lacked *wu wei* to guide them?

Movie buffs do not like to read reviews of films before they see them, so I will not spoil the reader's pleasures by noting how the *Tao Te Ching* develops the implications of *wu wei* for governance, warfare, commerce, and daily dealings. Instead I shall mention that, though I would not have written the five preceding paragraphs if I had not thought that they are basically on course, I am uneasy with the impression they might give that Taoism is a philosophic system. The *Tao Te Ching* is not a systematic book;

primary religious texts never are. They cannot be, for, designed to service people from every walk of life and temperament, they have no choice but to traffic in parables, analogies, intimations and allusions. Among other things, this precludes their having definitive translations, though I am confident that in the present case Professor Mair's translation will remain definitive for a long time, partly because he uses the Ma-wang-tui manuscripts, unearthed in 1973, which retire previous translations that worked from manuscripts that date five hundred years later. The compression and obscurity of archaic Chinese is daunting, with the result being that to read the *Tao Te Ching* is at the same time to interpret it. Professor Mair has done what he could for the reader, and I find his offering impressive. But in the end every reader must read his words, as he had to read his Chinese characters, in his own way.

To make matters worse, the text presents some specific problems that the reader should be alerted to. (I shall mention only one; Professor Mair calls attention to several others in his Afterword.) Several passages in the text seem to run counter to the book's general tenor, and occasionally—as in the assertion that "When the great Way was forsaken, there was humaneness and righteousness" (p. 80)—they make no sense at all. When the reader comes to those passages, I suggest that he not assume that the author has resorted to the trickster's device of using absurdities to blast us out of mental ruts. It makes more sense to side with the sinologists who simply assume that at these points the text is corrupt. After all, several centuries of copying went into even the Ma-wang-tui manuscripts, and mistakes do happen.

A second issue is more important. Did the *Tao Te Ching* intend to present itself as a freestanding outlook on life; or was its primary object to counterbalance certain Confucian excesses? (I am thinking of Confucianism's hierarchical structure, its bureaucracy, its anthropocentric focus, its stress on formal education with its linear thinking, and its pragmatic extroversion—let's all pitch in, pull up our socks, and get the job done.) It says nothing against Confucius's greatness to point out that no program can accomplish everything, and his program neglected regions of the Chinese psyche that could not be forever denied. The *Tao Te Ching* champions those regions persuasively. Balancing Confucius's stress on the group, the *Tao Te Ching* claims rights for the individual; complementing his call for social responsibility, it reminds us that our private lives—once characterized by a Russian writer as "picking one's nose while looking at the sunset"—deserve attention, too. When Le Corbusier remarked that "the Swiss are clean, and neat, and efficient, and to hell with them!" the authors of the *Tao Te Ching* would have understood completely. Confucian orthodoxy clamped over the individual a vise of social expectations so demanding that it almost, at times, had to trigger "the still small voice that mutters 'fiddlesticks.'" It is said that every Chinese bureaucrat was a Confucianist while he was in office, but if he lost his appointment his Taoist side came forward. One was likely to find him, canary cage in one hand and a volume of Li Po's poems in the other, heading for a tea shop in the hills where the springwater was known for making exceptionally fine tea.

That the *Tao Te Ching* has this "majesty's loyal opposition" side is undeniable; chapter 31 provides us with a clear example. But it would be going too far to suppose that without Confucianism to lean against, Taoism would fall on its face. Ultimately, it stands on its own feet, counseling a way of life that would have us enter more deeply into the world and overlap with it increasingly. With water again as its teacher, it invites us to see that much of our flailing in life's river stems from our thinking that we must labor mightily to stay afloat. We do not realize how much its water supports us of its own accord.

Especially in our time of ecological soul-searching, multitudes (I believe) will respond to the way this book— one of the most influential ever compiled—counters our anthropocentric tendencies and distrust by positioning our species in a vaster order of being and meaning than modernity currently accepts. Recognizing the extent to which our civilization is fatally out of balance with itself and the natural world, seeking a deeper and truer integration of human ways with the eternal way, such readers will find in this book a message of clarity and hope. "Heaven's net is vast;/Though its meshes are wide, nothing escapes" (p. 48).

# PREFACE

Next to the Bible and the *Bhagavad Gītā*, the *Tao Te Ching* is the most translated book in the world. Well over a hundred different renditions of the Taoist classic have been made into English alone, not to mention the dozens in German, French, Italian, Dutch, Latin, and other European languages. There are several reasons for the superabundance of translations. The first is that the *Tao Te Ching* is considered to be the fundamental text of both philosophical and religious Taoism. Indeed, the Tao, or Way, which is at the heart of the *Tao Te Ching*, is also the centerpiece of all Chinese religion and thought. Naturally, different schools and sects bring somewhat different slants to the Tao, but all subscribe to the notion that there is a single, overarching Way that encompasses everything in the universe. As such, the *Tao Te Ching* shares crucial points of similarity with other major religious scriptures the world over.

The second reason for the popularity of the *Tao Te Ching* is its brevity. There are few bona fide classics that are so short, yet so packed with food for thought. One can read and reread the *Tao Te Ching* scores of times without exhausting the insights it offers.

The third aspect that accounts for the wide repute of the *Tao Te Ching* is its deceptive simplicity: In the words of the author himself, it is supposedly "very easy to understand," when actually it is quite difficult to comprehend fully. Paradox is the essence of the *Tao Te Ching*, so much so that even scholars with a solid grounding in classical Chinese cannot be sure they have grasped what the Old Master is really saying in his pithy maxims. For this reason, I vowed two decades ago that I would never attempt to translate the *Tao Te Ching*. However, an unexpected event forced me to recant: The recent discovery of two ancient manuscripts in China made it possible to produce a totally new translation of the *Tao Te Ching* far more accurate and reliable than any published previously. These manuscripts are at least a half a millennium older than commonly translated versions.

This translation of the *Tao Te Ching* is based wholly on these new-found manuscripts. Their availability has made it possible to strip away the distortions and obfuscations of a tradition that has striven for two millennia to "improve" the text with commentaries and interpretations more amenable to various religious, philosophical, and political persuasions. And they have provided me with the means to make the translation in this book significantly different from all other previously existing translations.

In late 1973, when Chinese archaeologists working at Ma-wang-tui, in central China about a hundred miles south of the Yangtze River, unearthed two silk manuscripts of the *Tao Te Ching*, scholars of ancient China around the world were overjoyed. Forty-nine other important items, including the earliest extant version of the *Book of Changes*, were also found. It will be many years before sinologists fully absorb the wealth of new materials made available by the Ma-wang-tui manuscript finds, but we are already beginning to reap important benefits.

By relying on the Ma-wang-tui manuscripts for the present translation of the *Tao Te Ching*, I have solved a number of problems that have puzzled interpreters of the text for centuries. For example, line 8 of chapter 77 reads "To die but not be forgotten. . . ." In previously available editions of the *Tao Te Ching*, this read "To die but not perish . . . ," which does not really make sense even in a religious Taoist context. There are dozens of such instances where the Ma-wang-tui manuscripts are much more intelligible than the old standard editions, which are the basis of almost all other translations. I have pointed out several of these cases in the Notes.

The Ma-wang-tui manuscripts have also enabled me to make breakthroughs in determining the origin and composition of the text. In the Afterword and in my translation, I view the core of the *Tao Te Ching*, as having derived from oral tradition rather than from a single author. This characteristic is obscured by the explanatory comments in all other versions of the text and even more frequently by the use of misleading Chinese characters that has resulted from phonological change over the course of many centuries. Since the Ma-wang-tui manuscripts are much nearer to the date of the composition of the original *Tao Te Ching*, it is natural that they preserve more faithfully many of the features of the oral wisdom on which it was based.

Working on the relatively unstudied Ma-wang-tui manuscripts is more difficult than resorting to the ready solutions of the standard editions, which have been repeatedly commented upon and translated. It is also much more inspiring to come to grips with the Ma-wang-tui materials than to rehash the standard version yet again. One is conscious of being in the presence of manuscripts written close to the time when the *Tao Te Ching* crystallized as the foundation of both religious and philosophical Taoism. Without the discovery of the Ma-wang-tui manuscripts, I would never have been prompted to translate the *Tao Te Ching*; with them, reinterpreting the *Tao Te Ching* has become a stimulating challenge.

Once I assumed the task of creating an entirely fresh translation of the *Tao Te Ching*, I became preoccupied with endless details, such as how to convey the meaning of the second word in the title. I spent two full months trying to arrive at a satisfactory translation of *te*. Walking through the woods, riding on the train, buying groceries, chopping wood—the elusive notion of *te* was always on my mind. The final choice of "integrity" is based on a thorough etymological study of the word, together with a careful consideration of each of its forty-four occurrences in the text. In certain instances perhaps another word such as "self," "character," "personality," "virtue," "charisma," or "power" might have been more befitting. But "integrity" is the only word that seems plausible throughout. By "integrity," I mean the totality of an individual including his or her moral stance, whether good or bad.

We shall return to explore this concept in much greater depth in Part II of the Afterword, but I should like to add here that the Ma-wang-tui manuscripts were instrumental in helping me decide upon "integrity" as the right translation for *te* in the *Tao Te Ching*. In the first place, the archaic forms of the Chinese character for *te* used in the manuscripts caused me to realize that this term signified the holistic inner quality or character of a person. The basic components of the

Chinese graph at the time of the writing of the *Tao Te Ching* were an eye looking straight ahead, and the heart, and a sign for movement or behavior. Visually, these components are much clearer on the Ma-wang-tui manuscripts than they are in later stylized forms of the character for *te*, which become far more abstract and arbitrary. Secondly, several of the previously unknown texts among the Ma-wang-tui manuscripts, especially those dealing with metaphysical questions, also contain elaborate discussions of *te*. These, too, served to sharpen my appreciation of *te* as it was used in the intellectual milieu in which the *Tao Te Ching* took shape.

Whether seeking the right English word for *te* or coping with unusual Chinese graphs that were not to be found in any dictionary, my paramount guide has been historical linguistics. Only by the most rigorous application of this discipline can we hope to come close to a full understanding of ancient texts. At the same time I also sought inspiration from the muse so as not to betray the poetic beauty of the *Tao Te Ching*. My aim has been to create an authentic English version of the *Tao Te Ching* that is both eminently readable and sinologically precise. Because the original is in many places maddeningly obscure and frustratingly ambiguous, this was no mean task. Nonetheless, I am satisfied that the final result has been worth all the effort and that the present rendition comes closer than any other to affording someone who knows no classical Chinese the thought-provoking, mind-bending experience of reading the original.

An unusual feature of the present translation is its format. The layout of the words on the page is very carefully calculated to reflect the linguistic structure of the classical Chinese text. By paying attention to the arrangement of the words of the translation, the reader will be able to discern various grammatical, syntactical, and stylistic features of the original. Placement of particles, parallelism, antithesis, and so forth are all more or less evident in the physical appearance of the translation. Most, but not all, of the *Tao Te Ching* may be divided into rhymed sections. The rhyme schemes, in turn, fall into many different categories. Only occasionally do I employ rhyme in the translation, instead approximating its effects for the modern American reader by such devices as consonance, assonance, and other familiar poetic techniques.

The primary duty of the translator is to convey, as nearly as possible, a semblance of the original text in his or her own language. To do so, one must pay attention to form, content, style, diction, and sound. It is not enough merely to transfer the meaning of the original text; one also needs to replicate its effects. If a text is somewhat rough in places, one should resist the temptation to ameliorate it; if it is lyrical, one's own verse should sing. Because of the history of its composition, the style of the *Tao Te Ching* varies greatly. I have striven to recreate in my own rendition the various voices we hear speaking out of the past—the Taoist mystic, the political strategist, the utopian architect, the anti-Confucian philosopher, the clairvoyant poet, the meditative Yogin. If the reader is able to hear with any degree of fidelity more than one of the strains in this thought-provoking *concertstück*, my efforts will have been amply rewarded.

In the Afterword I again endeavor to break virgin territory. The first part shows how the *Tao Te Ching* represents the accumulated wisdom of centuries, not the enterprise of one author. As such, the real title of this book should be something like *Sayings of the Old Masters*. For the sake of convenience and familiarity, nonetheless, I continue to refer to it as the *Tao Te Ching*. The Afterword provides an etymological examination of the three words that make up the customary title of the book, together with explanations of the name of the presumed author and several other key terms.

Another radical departure from the past is my recognition of the *Tao Te Ching*'s intimate relationship to that other well-known oriental classic the *Bhagavad Gītā*. Having read both of them in their original languages repeatedly and attentively over the past two decades, I have come to believe that they are connected in an essential way. In the Afterword and Notes I have also discussed many similarities between Indian Yoga and Chinese Taoism, schools of religion and philosophy with which both books are closely associated.

At present there are only three conceivable explanations for how this relationship could have developed: (1) China borrowed the Yogic system and its attendant practices from India; (2) India borrowed Taoism and its attendant practices from China; (3) both India and China were the recipients of inspiration from a third source. Much research remains to be done, of course, before a conclusive answer can be given. We must also await the results of more thorough archaeological excavations, particularly in Sinkiang (the Chinese part of Central Asia), through which the famous silk roads passed, and along the southeast coast of China, where ships from India and Arabia regularly arrived. Nonetheless, presently available data indicate an Indian priority that can be traced back to at least the beginning of the first millennium B.C.

It is ultimately of little consequence whether Taoism is indebted to Yoga or Yoga to Taoism. What really matters is that they are both unique manifestations of a common human heritage. That is the light in which I have endeavored to view them in this little volume.

## ACKNOWLEDGMENT

I would like to thank my editor, Linda Loewenthal, for managing to be both gentle and firm in helping me to make this book more accessible to the people for whom it was written.

## NOTE ON THE
## NUMBERING OF CHAPTERS

The numbers running consecutively from 1 to 81 follow the sequence of the Ma-wang-tui manuscripts. The numbers in parentheses indicate the corresponding chapters of the previous standard text.

## NOTE ON THE
## USE OF PRONOUNS

The third person pronoun is often omitted in classical Chinese, but even when it is explicitly stated, rarely is the sense of gender implied. The translator not only has to supply a subject to satisfy the requirements of English grammar, but is forced to decide in each instance whether "he," "she," or "it" is more appropriate. To avoid overemphasis on the masculine, I have used impersonal or feminine pronouns for the third person whenever possible. When referring to the "sage king," however, I have had to use the masculine form because it is a simple fact of history that in ancient Chinese society this term always referred to men.

INTEGRITY

# 1
## (38)

The person of superior integrity
    does not insist upon his integrity;
For this reason, he has integrity.
The person of inferior integrity
    never loses sight of his integrity;
For this reason, he lacks integrity.

The person of superior integrity takes no action,
    nor has he a purpose for acting.
The person of superior humaneness takes action,
    but has no purpose for acting.
The person of superior righteousness takes action,
    and has a purpose for acting.
The person of superior etiquette takes action,
    but others do not respond to him;
Whereupon he rolls up his sleeves
    and coerces them.

Therefore,
    When the Way is lost,
        afterward comes integrity.
    When integrity is lost,
        afterward comes humaneness.
    When humaneness is lost,
        afterward comes righteousness.
    When righteousness is lost,
        afterward comes etiquette.

Now,
> Etiquette is the attenuation of trustworthiness,
> and the source of disorder.
> Foreknowledge is but the blossomy ornament of the Way,
> and the source of ignorance.

For this reason,
> The great man resides in substance,
> not in attenuation.
> He resides in fruitful reality,
> not in blossomy ornament.

Therefore,
> He rejects the one and adopts the other.

# 2
## (39)

---

In olden times, these attained unity:
    Heaven attained unity,
        and thereby became pure.
    Earth attained unity,
        and thereby became tranquil.
    The spirits attained unity,
        and thereby became divine.
    The valley attained unity,
        and thereby became full.
    Feudal lords and kings attained unity,
        and thereby all was put right.

Yet, pushed to the extreme,
It implies that,
    If heaven were ever pure,
        it would be likely to rend.
It implies that,
    If earth were ever tranquil,
        it would be likely to quake.
It implies that,
    If the spirits were ever divine,
        they would be likely to dissipate.
It implies that,
    If the valley were ever full,
        it would be likely to run dry.
It implies that,
    If feudal lords and kings were ever noble
        and thereby exalted,
      they would be likely to fall.

Therefore,
> It is necessary to be noble,
>> and yet take humility as a basis.
> It is necessary to be exalted,
>> and yet take modesty as a foundation.

Now, for this reason,
> Feudal lords and kings style themselves
>> "orphaned," "destitute," and "hapless."
> Is this not because they take humility as their basis?

Therefore,
> Striving for an excess of praise,
>> one ends up without praise.

Consequently,
> Desire not to be jingling as jade
>> nor stolid as stone.

# 3
## (41)

When the superior man hears the Way,
    he is scarcely able to put it into practice.
When the middling man hears the Way,
    he appears now to preserve it, now to lose it.
When the inferior man hears the Way,
    he laughs at it loudly.
If he did not laugh,
    it would not be fit to be the Way.

For this reason,
There is a series of epigrams that says:
    "The bright Way seems dim.
    The forward Way seems backward.
    The level Way seems bumpy.
    Superior integrity seems like a valley.
    The greatest whiteness seems grimy.
    Ample integrity seems insufficient.
    Robust integrity seems apathetic.
    Plain truth seems sullied.

    The great square has no corners.
    The great vessel is never completed.
    The great note sounds muted.
    The great image has no form.

    The Way is concealed and has no name."

Indeed,
    The Way alone is good at beginning
        and good at completing.

---

Reversal is the movement of the Way;
Weakness is the usage of the Way.

All creatures under heaven are born from being;
Being is born from nonbeing.

# 5
## (42)

The Way gave birth to unity,
Unity gave birth to duality,
Duality gave birth to trinity,
Trinity gave birth to the myriad creatures.

The myriad creatures bear yin on their backs
      and embrace yang in their bosoms.
They neutralize these vapors
      and thereby achieve harmony.

That which all under heaven hate most
Is to be orphaned, destitute, and hapless.
Yet kings and dukes call themselves thus.

Things may be diminished by being increased,
      increased by being diminished.

Therefore,
    That which people teach,
    After deliberation, I also teach people.

Therefore,
    "The tyrant does not die a natural death."
    I take this as my mentor.

# 6
## (43)

The softest thing under heaven
    gallops triumphantly over
The hardest thing under heaven.

Nonbeing penetrates nonspace.
Hence,
    I know the advantages of nonaction.

The doctrine without words,
The advantage of nonaction—
    few under heaven can realize these!

# 7
## (44)

---

Name or person,
     which is nearer?
Person or property,
     which is dearer?
Gain or loss,
     which is drearier?

Many loves entail great costs,
Many riches entail heavy losses.

Know contentment and you shall not be disgraced,
Know satisfaction and you shall not be imperiled;
     then you will long endure.

# 8
## (45)

---

Great perfection appears defective,
    but its usefulness is not diminished.
Great fullness appears empty,
    but its usefulness is not impaired.

Great straightness seems crooked,
Great cleverness seems clumsy,
Great triumph seems awkward.

Bustling about vanquishes cold,
Standing still vanquishes heat.

Pure and still,
    one can put things right everywhere under heaven.

# 9
## (46)

When the Way prevails under heaven,
swift horses are relegated to fertilizing fields.
When the Way does not prevail under heaven,
war-horses breed in the suburbs.

No guilt is greater than giving in to desire,
No disaster is greater than discontent,
No crime is more grievous than the desire for gain.

Therefore,
Contentment that derives from knowing
when to be content
is eternal contentment.

# 10
## (47)

Without going out-of-doors,
   one may know all under heaven;
Without peering through windows,
   one may know the Way of heaven.

The farther one goes,
The less one knows.

For this reason,
   The sage knows without journeying,
      understands without looking,
      accomplishes without acting.

# 11
## (48)

The pursuit of learning results in daily increase,
Hearing the Way leads to daily decrease.
Decrease and again decrease,
   until you reach nonaction.
Through nonaction,
   no action is left undone.

Should one desire to gain all under heaven,
One should remain ever free of involvements.
For,
   Just as surely as one becomes involved,
   One is unfit for gaining all under heaven.

# 12
## (49)

The sage never has a mind of his own;
He considers the minds of the common people to be his mind.

Treat well those who are good,
Also treat well those who are not good;
    thus is goodness attained.

Be sincere to those who are sincere,
Also be sincere to those who are insincere;
    thus is sincerity attained.

The sage
    is self-effacing in his dealings with all under heaven,
    and bemuddles his mind for the sake of all under heaven.

The common people all rivet their eyes and ears upon him,
And the sage makes them all chuckle like children.

# 13
## (50)

---

A person comes forth to life and enters into death.
Three out of ten are partners of life,
Three out of ten are partners of death,
And the people whose every movement leads them to the
        land of death because they cling to life
Are also three out of ten.

Now,
    What is the reason for this?
    It is because they cling to life.

Indeed,
I have heard that
    One who is good at preserving life
        does not avoid tigers and rhinoceroses
            when he walks in the hills;
        nor does he put on armor and take up weapons
            when he enters a battle.
    The rhinoceros has no place to jab its horn,
    The tiger has no place to fasten its claws,
    Weapons have no place to admit their blades.

Now,
    What is the reason for this?
    Because on him there are no mortal spots.

# 14
## (51)

The Way gives birth to them and integrity nurtures them.
Matter forms them and function completes them.

For this reason,
The myriad creatures respect the Way and esteem integrity.
Respect for the Way and esteem for integrity
are by no means conferred upon them
but always occur naturally.

The Way gives birth to them,
nurtures them,
rears them,
follows them,
shelters them,
toughens them,
sustains them,
protects them.
It gives birth but does not possess,
acts but does not presume,
rears but does not control.

This is what is called "mysterious integrity."

# 15
## (52)

Everything under heaven has a beginning
　　which may be thought of as the mother
　　　　of all under heaven.
Having realized the mother,
　　you thereby know her children.
Knowing her children,
　　go back to abide with the mother.
To the end of your life,
　　you will not be imperiled.

Stopple the orifices of your heart,
Close your doors;
　　your whole life you will not suffer.
Open the gate of your heart,
Meddle with affairs;
　　your whole life you will be beyond salvation.

Seeing what is small is called insight,
Abiding in softness is called strength.

Use your light to return to insight,
Be not an inheritor of personal calamity.

This is called "following the constant."

# 16
## (53)

If I were possessed of the slightest knowledge,
    traveling on the great Way,
My only fear would be to go astray.
The great Way is quite level,
    but the people are much enamored of mountain trails.

The court is thoroughly deserted,
The fields are choked with weeds,
The granaries are altogether empty.

Still there are some who
    wear clothes with fancy designs and brilliant colors,
    sharp swords hanging at their sides,
    are sated with food,
    overflowing with possessions and wealth.

This is called "the brazenness of a bandit."
The brazenness of a bandit is surely not the Way!

# 17
## (54)

What is firmly established cannot be uprooted;
What is tightly embraced cannot slip away.

Thus sacrificial offerings made by sons and grandsons
will never end.

Cultivated in the person, integrity is true.
Cultivated in the family, integrity is ample.
Cultivated in the village, integrity lasts long.
Cultivated in the state, integrity is abundant.
Cultivated everywhere under heaven, integrity is vast.

Observe other persons through your own person.
Observe other families through your own family.
Observe other villages through your own village.
Observe other states through your own state.
Observe all under heaven through all under heaven.

How do I know the nature of all under heaven?
Through this.

# 18
## (55)
---

He who embodies the fullness of integrity
    is like a ruddy infant.

Wasps, spiders, scorpions, and snakes
    will not sting or bite him;
Rapacious birds and fierce beasts
    will not seize him.

His bones are weak and his sinews soft,
    yet his grip is tight.
He knows not the joining of male and female,
    yet his penis is aroused.
His essence has reached a peak.

He screams the whole day without becoming hoarse;
His harmony has reached perfection.

Harmony implies constancy;
Constancy requires insight.

Striving to increase one's life is ominous;
To control the vital breath with one's mind entails force.

Something that grows old while still in its prime
    is said to be not in accord with the Way;
Not being in accord with the Way
    leads to an early demise.

# 19
## (56)

One who knows does not speak;
One who speaks does not know.

He
Stopples the openings of his heart,
Closes his doors,
Diffuses the light,
Mingles with the dust,
Files away his sharp points,
Unravels his tangles.

This is called "mysterious identity."

Therefore,
Neither can one attain intimacy with him,
Nor can one remain distant from him;
Neither can one profit from him,
Nor can one be harmed by him;
Neither can one achieve honor through him,
Nor can one be debased by him.

Therefore,
He is esteemed by all under heaven.

# 20
## (57)

Rule the state with uprightness,
Deploy your troops with craft,
Gain all under heaven with noninterference.

How do I know this is actually so?

Now,
    The more taboos under heaven,
      the poorer the people;
    The more clever devices people have,
      the more confused the state and ruling house;
    The more knowledge people have,
      the more strange things spring up;
    The more legal affairs are given prominence,
      the more numerous bandits and thieves.

For this reason,
The sage has a saying:
    "I take no action,
      yet the people transform themselves;
    I am fond of stillness,
      yet the people correct themselves;
    I do not interfere in affairs,
      yet the people enrich themselves;
    I desire not to desire,
      yet the people of themselves become
        simple as unhewn logs."

# 21
## (58)

When government is anarchic,
   the people are honest;
When government is meddlesome,
   the state is lacking.

Disaster is that whereon good fortune depends,
Good fortune is that wherein disaster lurks.
   Who knows their limits?

When there is no uprightness,
   correct reverts to crafty,
   good reverts to gruesome.

The delusion of mankind,
How long have been its days!

For this reason, be
   Square but not cutting,
   Angular but not prickly,
   Straight but not arrogant,
   Bright but not dazzling.

# 22
## (59)

To rule men and serve heaven,
    there is nothing like thrift.
Now,
    Only through thrift
      can one be prepared;
    Being prepared
      means having a heavy store of integrity;
    With a heavy store of integrity,
      he can overcome everything.
    Able to overcome everything,
      no one knows his limits;
    If no one knows his limits,
      he can have the kingdom;
    Having the mother of the kingdom,
      he can long endure.
    This is called "sinking roots firm and deep,
      the Way of long life and lasting vision."

# 23
## (60)

Ruling a big kingdom is like cooking a small fish.
If one oversees all under heaven in accord with the Way,
   demons have no spirit.
It is not that the demons have no spirit,
   but that their spirits do not harm people.
It is not merely that their spirits do not harm people,
   but that the sage also does not harm them.

Now,
   When neither harms the other,
      integrity accrues to both.

# 24
## (61)

A large state is like a low-lying estuary,
    the female of all under heaven.
In the congress of all under heaven,
    the female always conquers the male through her stillness.
Because she is still,
    it is fitting for her to lie low.
By lying beneath a small state,
    a large state can take over a small state.
By lying beneath a large state,
    a small state can be taken over by a large state.

Therefore,
    One may either take over or be taken over by lying low.

Therefore,
    The large state wishes only to annex and nurture others;
    The small state wants only to join with and serve others.

Now,
    Since both get what they want,
    It is fitting for the large state to lie low.

The Way is the cistern of the myriad creatures;
It is the treasure of the good man,
And that which is treasured by the bad man.

Beautiful words can be traded,
Noble deeds can be used as gifts for others.
Why should we reject even what is bad about men?

Therefore,
    When the son of heaven is enthroned
        or the three ministers are installed,
    Although they may have large jade disks
    And be preceded by teams of four horses,
    It would be better for them to sit down
        and make progress in this.

What was the reason for the ancients
    to value this so highly?
Did they not say:
    "Seek and thou shalt receive;
    Sin and thou shalt be forgiven"?

Therefore,
    It is valued by all under heaven.

# 26
## (63)

Act through nonaction,
Handle affairs through noninterference,
Taste what has no taste,
Regard the small as great, the few as many,
Repay resentment with integrity.

Undertake difficult tasks
    by approaching what is easy in them;
Do great deeds
    by focusing on their minute aspects.

All difficulties under heaven arise from what is easy,
All great things under heaven arise from what is minute.

For this reason,
    The sage never strives to do what is great.
Therefore,
    He can achieve greatness.

One who lightly assents
    will seldom be believed;
One who thinks everything is easy
    will encounter much difficulty.

For this reason,
    Even the sage considers things difficult.
Therefore,
    In the end he is without difficulty.

# 27
## (64)

What is secure is easily grasped,
What has no omens is easily forestalled,
What is brittle is easily split,
What is minuscule is easily dispersed.

Act before there is a problem;
Bring order before there is disorder.

A tree that fills the arms' embrace
   is born from a downy shoot;
A terrace nine layers high
   starts from a basketful of earth;
An ascent of a hundred strides
   begins beneath one's foot.

Who acts fails;
Who grasps loses.

For this reason,
   The sage does not act.
Therefore,
   He does not fail.

   He does not grasp.
Therefore,
   He does not lose.

In pursuing their affairs,
　　people often fail when they are close to success.
Therefore,
　　If one is as cautious at the end as at the beginning,
　　there will be no failures.

For this reason,
　　The sage desires to be without desire
　　　and does not prize goods that are hard to obtain;
　　He learns not to learn
　　　and reverts to what the masses pass by.

　　Thus, he can help the myriad creatures be natural,
　　　but dares not act.

# 28
## (65)

The ancients who practiced the Way
   did not enlighten the people with it;
They used it, rather, to stupefy them.

The people are hard to rule
   because they have too much knowledge.
Therefore,
   Ruling a state through knowledge is to rob the state;
   Ruling a state through ignorance
      brings integrity to the state.

One who is always mindful of these two types
      grasps a paradigm;
Mindfulness of this paradigm is called "mysterious integrity."

Deep and distant is this mysterious integrity!
It runs counter to things
   until it reaches the great confluence.

The river and sea can be kings of
     the hundred valley streams
     because they are good at lying below them.
For this reason,
     They can be kings of the hundred valley streams.
For this reason, too,
     If the sage wants to be above the people,
          in his words, he must put himself below them;
     If he wishes to be before the people,
          in his person, he must stand behind them.
Therefore,
     He is situated in front of the people,
          but they are not offended;
     He is situated above the people,
          but they do not consider him a burden.
     All under heaven happily push him forward without
          wearying.
     Is this not because he is without contention?
Therefore,
     No one under heaven can contend with him.

# 30
## (80)

Let there be a small state with few people,
    where military devices find no use;
Let the people look solemnly upon death,
    and banish the thought of moving elsewhere.

They may have carts and boats,
    but there is no reason to ride them;
They may have armor and weapons,
    but they have no reason to display them.

Let the people go back to tying knots
    to keep records.
Let their food be savory,
    their clothes beautiful,
    their customs pleasurable,
    their dwellings secure.

Though they may gaze across at a neighboring state,
    and hear the sounds of its dogs and chickens,
The people will never travel back and forth,
    till they die of old age.

# 31
## (81)

Sincere words are not beautiful,
Beautiful words are not sincere.
He who knows is not learned,
He who is learned does not know.
He who is good does not have much,
He who has much is not good.

The sage does not hoard.
The more he does for others,
    the more he has himself;
The more he gives to others,
    the more his own bounty increases.

Therefore,
    The Way of heaven benefits but does not harm,
    The Way of man acts but does not contend.

All under heaven say that I am great,
   great but unconventional.
Now,
   Precisely because I am unconventional,
      I can be great;
   If I were conventional,
      I would long since have become a trifle.

   I have always possessed three treasures
      that I guard and cherish.
   The first is compassion,
   The second is frugality,
   The third is not daring to be ahead of all under heaven.

Now,
   Because I am compassionate,
      I can be brave;
   Because I am frugal,
      I can be magnanimous;
   Because I dare not be ahead of all under heaven,
      I can be a leader in the completion of affairs.

If, today, I were to
   Be courageous while forsaking compassion,
   Be magnanimous while forsaking frugality,
   Get ahead while forsaking the hindmost,
      that would be death!

For compassion
   In war brings victory,
   In defense brings invulnerability.

Whomsoever heaven would establish,
   It surrounds with a bulwark of compassion.

# 33
## (68)

A good warrior is not bellicose,
A good fighter does not anger,
A good conqueror does not contest his enemy,
One who is good at using others puts himself below them.
This is called "integrity without competition,"
This is called "using others,"
This is called "parity with heaven,"
    —the pinnacle of the ancients.

# 34
## (69)

The strategists have a saying:
    "I dare not be host,
        but would rather be guest;
    I advance not an inch,
        but instead retreat a foot."

This is called
    Marching without ranks,
    Bearing nonexistent arms,
    Flourishing nonexistent weapons,
    Driving back nonexistent enemies.

    There is no greater misfortune
        than not having a worthy foe;
    Once I believe there are no worthy foes,
        I have well-nigh forfeited my treasures.

Therefore,
    When opposing forces are evenly matched,
    The one who is saddened will be victorious.

# 35
## (70)

My words are
  very easy to understand,
  very easy to practice.
But no one is able to understand them,
And no one is able to practice them.

Words have authority.
Affairs have an ancestry.

It is simply because of their ignorance,
  that they do not understand me;
Those who understand me are few,
  thus I am ennobled.

For this reason,
  The sage wears coarse clothing over his shoulders,
  but carries jade within his bosom.

# 36
## (71)

To realize that you do not understand is a virtue;
Not to realize that you do not understand is a defect.

The reason why
The sage has no defects,
Is because he treats defects as defects.

Thus,
He has no defects.

When the people do not fear the majestic,
Great majesty will soon visit them.

Do not limit their dwellings,
Do not suppress their livelihood.
Simply because you do not suppress them,
they will not grow weary of you.

For this reason,
The sage is self-aware,
but does not flaunt himself;
He is self-devoted,
but does not glorify himself.

Therefore,
He rejects the one and adopts the other.

# 38
## (73)

He who is brave in daring will be killed,
He who is brave in not daring will survive.
One of these two courses is beneficial,
The other is harmful.

Who knows the reason for heaven's dislikes?
The Way of heaven
    does not war
        yet is good at conquering,
    does not speak
        yet is good at answering,
    is not summoned
        yet comes of itself,
    is relaxed
        yet good at making plans.

Heaven's net is vast;
Though its meshes are wide,
    nothing escapes.

# 39
## (74)

---

If the people never fear death,
what is the purpose of threatening to kill them?
If the people ever fear death,
and I were to capture and kill those who are devious,
who would dare to be so?
If the people must be ever fearful of death,
then there will always be an executioner.

Now,
To kill in place of the executioner
Is like
Hewing wood in place of the master carpenter;
Few indeed will escape cutting their own hands!

# 40
## (75)

———————

Human hunger
    is the result of overtaxation.
For this reason,
    There is hunger.

The common people are not governable
    because of their superiors' actions.
For this reason,
    They are not governable.

The people make light of death
    because of too much emphasis on the quest for life.
For this reason,
    They make light of death.

Now,
    Only she who acts not for the sake of life
    Is wiser than those who value life highly.

# 41
## (76)

Human beings are
   soft and supple when alive,
   stiff and straight when dead.

The myriad creatures, the grasses and trees are
   soft and fragile when alive,
   dry and withered when dead.

Therefore, it is said:
   The rigid person is a disciple of death;
   The soft, supple, and delicate are lovers of life.

An army that is inflexible will not conquer;
A tree that is inflexible will snap.

The unyielding and mighty shall be brought low;
The soft, supple, and delicate will be set above.

# 42
## (77)

---

The Way of heaven is like the bending of a bow—
    the upper part is pressed down,
    the lower part is raised up,
    the part that has too much is reduced,
    the part that has too little is increased.
Therefore,
    The Way of heaven
        reduces surplus to make up for scarcity;
    The Way of man
        reduces scarcity and pays tribute to surplus.

Who is there that can have a surplus
    and take from it to pay tribute to heaven?
Surely only one who has the Way!

For this reason,
    The sage
        acts but does not possess,
        completes his work but does not dwell on it.
    In this fashion,
        he has no desire to display his worth.

# 43
## (78)

Nothing under heaven is softer or weaker than water,
and yet nothing is better
for attacking what is hard and strong,
because of its immutability.

The defeat of the hard by the soft,
The defeat of the strong by the weak—
this is known to all under heaven,
yet no one is able to practice it.

Therefore, in the words of the sage, it is said:
"He who bears abuse directed against the state
is called 'lord of the altars for the gods of soil and grain';
He who bears the misfortunes of the state
is called the 'king of all under heaven.' "

True words seem contradictory.

# 44
## (79)

Compromise with great resentment
will surely yield lingering resentment;
How can this be seen as good?

For this reason,
The sage holds the debtor's side of a contract
and does not make claims upon others.

Therefore,
The man of integrity attends to his debts;
The man without integrity attends to his exactions.

The Way of heaven is impartial,
yet is always with the good person.

# TAO

## THE WAY

# 45
## (1)

The ways that can be walked are not the eternal Way;
The names that can be named are not the eternal name.
The nameless is the origin of the myriad creatures;
The named is the mother of the myriad creatures.

Therefore,
> Always be without desire
>> in order to observe its wondrous subtleties;
> Always have desire
>> so that you may observe its manifestations.

Both of these derive from the same source;
They have different names but the same designation.

Mystery of mysteries,
The gate of all wonders!

When all under heaven know beauty as beauty,
   already there is ugliness;
When everyone knows goodness,
   this accounts for badness.

Being and nonbeing give birth to each other,
Difficult and easy complete each other,
Long and short form each other,
High and low fulfill each other,
Tone and voice harmonize with each other,
Front and back follow each other—
   it is ever thus.

For these reasons,
   The sage
      dwells in affairs of nonaction,
      carries out a doctrine without words.
   He lets the myriad creatures rise up
      but does not instigate them;
   He acts
      but does not presume;
   He completes his work
      but does not dwell on it.

Now,
   Simply because he does not dwell on them,
      his accomplishments never leave him.

# 47
## (3)

Not exalting men of worth
    prevents the people from competing;
Not putting high value on rare goods
    prevents the people from being bandits;
Not displaying objects of desire
    prevents the people from being disorderly.

For these reasons,
    The sage, in ruling,
        hollows their hearts,
        stuffs their stomachs,
        weakens their wills,
        builds up their bones,
    Always causing the people
        to be without knowledge and desire.
    He ensures that
        the knowledgeable dare not be hostile,
            and that is all.
Thus,
    His rule is universal.

# 48
## (4)

The Way is empty,
      yet never refills with use;
Bottomless it is,
      like the forefather of the myriad creatures.
It files away sharp points,
    unravels tangles,
    diffuses light,
    mingles with the dust.
Submerged it lies,
      seeming barely to subsist.
I know not whose child it is,
      only that it resembles the predecessor of God.

# 49
## (5)

Heaven and earth are inhumane;
    they view the myriad creatures as straw dogs.
The sage is inhumane;
    he views the common people as straw dogs.

The space between heaven and earth,
    how like a bellows it is!
Empty but never exhausted,
The more it pumps, the more comes out.

Hearing too much leads to utter exhaustion;
Better to remain in the center.

## 50
### (6)

The valley spirit never dies—
  it is called "the mysterious female";
The gate of the mysterious female
  is called "the root of heaven and earth."
Gossamer it is,
  seemingly insubstantial,
   yet never consumed through use.

# 51
## (7)

---

Heaven is long and earth is lasting.
Heaven and earth can be long and lasting
  because they do not live for themselves.
Therefore,
  They can be long-lived.

For this reason,
  The sage
    withdraws himself
      but comes to the fore,
    alienates himself
      but is always present.

  Is this not because he is free of private interests?
Therefore,
  He can accomplish his private interests.

# 52
## (8)

The highest good is like water;
Water is good at benefiting the myriad creatures
        but also struggles
    to occupy the place loathed by the masses.
Therefore,
    It is near to the Way.

The quality of an abode is in its location,
The quality of the heart is in its depths,
The quality of giving lies in trust,
The quality of correct governance lies in orderly rule,
The quality of an enterprise depends on ability,
The quality of movement depends on timing.

Now,
    It is precisely because one does not compete
        that there is no blame.

# 53
## (9)

Instead of keeping a bow taut while holding it straight,
    better to relax.
You may temper a sword until it is razor sharp,
    but you cannot preserve the edge for long.
When gold and jade fill your rooms,
    no one will be able to guard them for you.
If wealth and honor make you haughty,
    you bequeath misfortune upon yourself.
To withdraw when your work is finished,
    that is the Way of heaven.

# 54
## (10)

---

While you
> Cultivate the soul and embrace unity,
>> can you keep them from separating?
> Focus your vital breath until it is supremely soft,
>> can you be like a baby?
> Cleanse the mirror of mysteries,
>> can you make it free of blemish?
> Love the people and enliven the state,
>> can you do so without cunning?
> Open and close the gate of heaven,
>> can you play the part of the female?
> Reach out with clarity in all directions,
>> can you refrain from action?

It gives birth to them and nurtures them,
It gives birth to them but does not possess them,
It rears them but does not control them.
> This is called "mysterious integrity."

# 55
## (11)

Thirty spokes converge on a single hub,
   but it is in the space where there is nothing
   that the usefulness of the cart lies.
Clay is molded to make a pot,
   but it is in the space where there is nothing
   that the usefulness of the clay pot lies.
Cut out doors and windows to make a room,
   but it is in the spaces where there is nothing
   that the usefulness of the room lies.
Therefore,
   Benefit may be derived from something,
   but it is in nothing that we find usefulness.

# 56
## (12)

The five colors
   make a man's eyes blind;
Horseracing and hunting
   make a man's mind go mad;
Goods that are hard to obtain
   make a man's progress falter;
The five flavors
   make a man's palate dull;
The five tones
   make a man's ears deaf.

For these reasons,
   In ruling, the sage
      attends to the stomach, not to the eye.
Therefore,
   He rejects the one and adopts the other.

_____

"Being favored is so disgraceful that it startles,
Being honored is an affliction as great as one's body."

What is the meaning of
"Being favored is so disgraceful that it startles"?

Favor is debasing;
To find it is startling,
To lose it is startling.

This is the meaning of
"Being favored is so disgraceful that it startles."

What is the meaning of
"Being honored is an affliction as great as one's body"?

The reason I suffer great afflictions is because I have a body;
If I had no body, what affliction could I suffer?

Therefore,
When a man puts more emphasis on caring for his body
than on caring for all under heaven,
then all under heaven can be entrusted to him.
When a man is sparing of his body in caring
for all under heaven,
then all under heaven can be delivered to him.

# 58
## (14)

---

We look for it but do not see it;
 we name it "subtle."
We listen for it but do not hear it;
 we name it "rare."
We grope for it but do not grasp it;
 we name it "serene."

These three cannot be fully fathomed,
Therefore,
 They are bound together to make unity.

Of unity,
 its top is not distant,
 its bottom is not blurred.
Infinitely extended
 and unnameable,
It returns to nonentity.
This is called
 "the form of the formless,
 the image of nonentity."
This is called "the amorphous."

Following behind it,
 you cannot see its back;
Approaching it from the front,
 you cannot see its head.

Hold to the Way of today
   to manage the actualities of today,
   thereby understanding the primeval beginning.
This is called "the thread of the Way."

# 59
## (15)

Those of old who were adept in the Way
    were subtly profound and mysteriously perceptive,
So deep
    they could not be recognized.

Now,
    Because they could not be recognized,
One can describe their appearance only with effort:
    hesitant,
        as though crossing a stream in winter;
    cautious,
        as though fearful of their neighbors all around;
    solemn,
        as though guests in someone else's house;
    shrinking,
        as ice when it melts;
    plain,
        as an unhewn log;
    muddled,
        as turbid waters;
    expansive,
        as a broad valley.

If turbid waters are stilled,
    they will gradually become clear;
If something inert is set in motion,
    it will gradually come to life.

Those who preserved this Way did not wish to be full.
Now,
Simply because they did not wish to be full,
they could be threadbare and incomplete.

# 60
## (16)

___

Attain utmost emptiness,
Maintain utter stillness.

The myriad creatures arise side by side,
    thus I observe their renewal.
Heaven's creatures abound,
    but each returns to its roots,
        which is called "stillness."
This is termed "renewal of fate."
Renewal of fate is perpetual—
To know the perpetual is to be enlightened;
Not to know the perpetual is to be reckless—
    recklessness breeds evil.
To know the perpetual is to be tolerant—
    tolerance leads to ducal impartiality,
    ducal impartiality to kingliness,
    kingliness to heaven,
    heaven to the Way,
    the Way to permanence.

To the end of his days,
    he will not be imperiled.

# 61
## (17)

Preeminent is one whose subjects barely know he exists;
The next is one to whom they feel close and praise;
The next is one whom they fear;
The lowest is one whom they despise.

When the ruler's trust is wanting,
  there will be no trust in him.
Cautious,
  he values his words.
When his work is completed and his affairs finished,
  the common people say,
    "We are like this by ourselves."

# 62
## (18)

Therefore,
  When the great Way was forsaken,
    there was humaneness and righteousness;
  When cunning and wit appeared,
    there was great falsity;
  When the six family relationships lacked harmony,
    there were filial piety and parental kindness;
  When the state and royal house were in disarray,
    there were upright ministers.

# 63
## (19)

"Abolish sagehood and abandon cunning,
   the people will benefit a hundredfold;
Abolish humaneness and abandon righteousness,
   the people will once again be filial and kind;
Abolish cleverness and abandon profit,
   bandits and thieves will be no more."

These three statements
   are inadequate as a civilizing doctrine;
Therefore,
   Let something be added to them:

Evince the plainness of undyed silk,
Embrace the simplicity of the unhewn log;
Lessen selfishness,
Diminish desires;
Abolish learning
   and you will be without worries.

# 64
## (20)

Between "yes sir" and "certainly not!"
    how much difference is there?
Between beauty and ugliness,
    how great is the distinction?

He whom others fear,
    likewise cannot but fear others.

How confusing,
    there is no end to it all!

Joyful are the masses,
    as though feasting after the great sacrifice of oxen,
    or mounting a terrace in spring.

Motionless am I,
    without any sign,
    as a baby that has yet to gurgle.
How dejected!
    as though having nowhere to return.

The masses all have more than enough;
I alone am bereft.

I have the heart of a fool.
How muddled!

The ordinary man is luminously clear,
I alone seem confused.
The ordinary man is searchingly exact,
I alone am vague and uncertain.

How nebulous!
    as the ocean;
How blurred!
    as though without boundary.

The masses all have a purpose,
I alone am stubborn and uncouth.

I desire to be uniquely different from others
    by honoring the mother who nourishes.

# 65
## (21)

The appearance of grand integrity
    is that it follows the Way alone.
The Way objectified
    is blurred and nebulous.

How nebulous and blurred!
Yet within it there are images.
How blurred and nebulous!
Yet within it there are objects.
How cavernous and dark!
Yet within it there is an essence.
Its essence is quite real;
Within it there are tokens.

From the present back to the past,
Its name has been imperishable.
Through it we conform to the father of the masses.

How do I know what the father of the masses is like?
Through this.

# 66
## (24)

Who is puffed up cannot stand,
Who is self-absorbed has no distinction,
Who is self-revealing does not shine,
Who is self-assertive has no merit,
Who is self-praising does not last long.

As for the Way, we may say these are
  "excess provisions and extra baggage."
Creation abhors such extravagances.

Therefore,
  One who aspires to the Way,
    does not abide in them.

# 67
## (22)

---

If it
> is bent,
> > it will be preserved intact;
> is crooked,
> > it will be straightened;
> is sunken,
> > it will be filled;
> is worn-out,
> > it will be renewed;
> has little,
> > it will gain;
> has much,
> > it will be confused.

For these reasons,
> The sage holds on to unity
> > and serves as the shepherd of all under heaven.
> He is not self-absorbed,
> > therefore he shines forth;
> He is not self-revealing,
> > therefore he is distinguished;
> He is not self-assertive,
> > therefore he has merit;
> He does not praise himself,
> > therefore he is long-lasting.

Now,

    Simply because he does not compete,
    No one can compete with him.

    The old saying about the bent being preserved intact
    is indeed close to the mark!

    Truly, he shall be returned intact.

# 68
## (23)

To be sparing of speech is natural.

A whirlwind does not last the whole morning,
A downpour does not last the whole day.
Who causes them?
If even heaven and earth cannot cause them to persist,
   how much less can human beings?

Therefore,
   In pursuing his affairs,
      a man of the Way identifies with the Way,
      a man of integrity identifies with integrity,
      a man who fails identifies with failure.

   To him who identifies with integrity,
      the Way awards integrity;
   To him who identifies with failure,
      the Way awards failure.

# 69
## (25)

There was something featureless yet complete,
    born before heaven and earth;
Silent—amorphous—
    it stood alone and unchanging.

We may regard it as the mother of heaven and earth.
Not knowing its name,
    I style it the "Way."
If forced to give it a name,
    I would call it "great."
Being great implies flowing ever onward,
Flowing ever onward implies far-reaching,
Far-reaching implies reversal.

The Way is great,
Heaven is great,
Earth is great,
The king, too, is great.

Within the realm there are four greats,
    and the king is one among them.

Man
    patterns himself on earth,
Earth
    patterns itself on heaven,
Heaven
    patterns itself on the Way,
The Way
    patterns itself on nature.

# 70
## (26)

---

Heavy is the root of light;
Calm is the ruler of haste.

For these reasons,
    The superior man may travel the whole day
      without leaving his heavy baggage cart.
    Though inside the courtyard walls of a noisy inn,
      he placidly rises above it all.

    How then should a king with ten thousand chariots
      conduct himself lightly before all under heaven?

If he treats himself lightly,
    he will lose the taproot;
If he is hasty,
    he will lose the rulership.

# 71
## (27)

He who is skilled at traveling
    leaves neither tracks nor traces;
He who is skilled at speaking
    is flawless in his delivery;
He who is skilled in computation
    uses neither tallies nor counters;
He who is skilled at closing things tightly
    has neither lock nor key,
        but what he closes cannot be opened;
He who is good at binding
    has neither cord nor string,
        but what he binds cannot be untied.

For these reasons,
    The sage
        is always skilled at saving others
           and does not abandon them,
               nor does he abandon resources.
    This is called "inner intelligence."

Therefore,
    Good men are teachers for the good man,
    Bad men are foils for the good man.
    He who values not his teacher
        and loves not his foil,
    Though he be knowledgeable,
        is greatly deluded.

This is called "the wondrous essential."

# 72
## (28)

Know masculinity,
Maintain femininity,
  and be a ravine for all under heaven.
By being a ravine for all under heaven,
Eternal integrity will never desert you.
If eternal integrity never deserts you,
You will return to the state of infancy.

Know you are innocent,
Remain steadfast when insulted,
  and be a valley for all under heaven.
By being a valley for all under heaven,
Eternal integrity will suffice.
If eternal integrity suffices,
You will return to the simplicity of the unhewn log.

Know whiteness,
Maintain blackness,
  and be a model for all under heaven.
By being a model for all under heaven,
Eternal integrity will not err.
If eternal integrity does not err,
You will return to infinity.

When the unhewn log is sawn apart,
  it is made into tools;
When the sage is put to use,
  he becomes the chief of officials.

For

  Great carving does no cutting.

Of those who wish to take hold of all-under-heaven
and act upon it,
I have seen that they do not succeed.
Now,
All-under-heaven is a sacred vessel,
Not something that can be acted upon;
Who acts upon it will be defeated,
Who grasps it will lose it.

Of creatures,
some march forward, others follow behind;
some are shiveringly silent, others are all puffed up;
some are strong, others are meek;
some pile up, others collapse.

For these reasons,
The sage
rejects extremes,
rejects excess,
rejects extravagance.

# 74
## (30)

---

One who assists the ruler of men with the Way
    does not use force of arms against all under heaven;
Such a course is likely to boomerang.

Where armies have been stationed,
    briars and brambles will grow.

A good general fulfills his purpose
    and that is all.
He does not use force
    to seize for himself.

He fulfills his purpose,
    but is not proud;
He fulfills his purpose,
    but is not boastful;
He fulfills his purpose,
    but does not brag;
He fulfills his purpose
    only because he has no other choice.

This is called "fulfilling one's purpose without using force."

If something grows old while still in its prime,
This is called "not being in accord with the Way."
Not being in accord with the Way
    leads to an early demise.

# 75
## (31)

___

Now,
> Weapons are instruments of evil omen;
> Creation abhors them.

Therefore,
> One who aspires to the Way
>> does not abide in them.

> The superior man
>> at home honors the left,
>> on the battlefield honors the right.

Therefore,
> Weapons are not instruments of the superior man;
> Weapons are instruments of evil omen,
>> to be used only when there is no other choice.

> He places placidity above all
>> and refuses to prettify weapons;
> If one prettifies weapons,
>> this is to delight in the killing of others.

Now,
> One who delights in the killing of others
> Cannot exercise his will over all under heaven.

For this reason,
> On occasions for celebration,
>> the left is given priority;
> On occasions for mourning,
>> the right is given priority.

Therefore,
  A deputy general stands on the left,
  The general-in-chief stands on the right.
In other words,
  They stand in accordance with mourning ritual.

  The killing of masses of human beings,
    we bewail with sorrow and grief;
  Victory in battle,
    we commemorate with mourning ritual.

The Way is eternally nameless.

Though the unhewn log is small,
No one in the world dares subjugate it.
If feudal lords and kings could maintain it,
The myriad creatures would submit of themselves.

Heaven and earth unite
    to suffuse sweet dew.
Without commanding the people,
    equality will naturally ensue.

As soon as one begins to divide things up,
    there are names;
Once there are names,
    one should also know when to stop;
Knowing when to stop,
    one thereby avoids peril.

In metaphorical terms,
    The relationship of all under heaven to the Way
      is like that of valley streams
        to the river and sea.

# 77

## (33)

Understanding others is knowledge,
Understanding oneself is enlightenment;
Conquering others is power,
Conquering oneself is strength;
Contentment is wealth,
Forceful conduct is willfulness;
Not losing one's rightful place is to endure,
To die but not be forgotten is longevity.

# 78
## (34)

Rippling is the Way, flowing left and right!
Its tasks completed, its affairs finished,
Still it does not claim them for its own.
The myriad creatures return to it,
But it does not act as their ruler.

Eternally without desire,
It may be named among the small;
The myriad creatures return to it,
But it does not act as their ruler;
It may be named among the great.

For these reasons,
    The sage can achieve greatness,
    Because he does not act great.
Therefore,
    He can achieve greatness.

Hold fast to the great image
  and all under heaven will come;
They will
  come but not be harmed,
  rest in safety and peace;
Music and fine food
  will make the passerby halt.

Therefore,
  When the Way is expressed verbally,
  We say such things as
    "how bland and tasteless it is!"
  "We look for it,
    but there is not enough to be seen."
  "We listen for it,
    but there is not enough to be heard."
  Yet, when put to use,
    it is inexhaustible!

# 80
## (36)

When you wish to contract something,
 you must momentarily expand it;
When you wish to weaken something,
 you must momentarily strengthen it;
When you wish to reject something,
 you must momentarily join with it;
When you wish to seize something,
 you must momentarily give it up.
This is called "subtle insight."

The soft and weak conquer the strong.

Fish cannot be removed from the watery depths;
The profitable instruments of state
   cannot be shown to the people.

# 81
## (37)

The Way is eternally nameless.
If feudal lords and kings preserve it,
The myriad creatures will be transformed by themselves.
After transformation, if they wish to rise up,
I shall restrain them with the nameless unhewn log.
By restraining them with the nameless unhewn log,
They will not feel disgraced;
Not feeling disgraced,
They will be still,
Whereupon heaven and earth will be made right by themselves.

# NOTES AND COMMENTARY

1.7—**humaneness** Like "righteousness" and "etiquette" in lines 9 and 11 below, this is an important element of Confucian ideology. It is obvious that the author of this chapter takes a rather dim view of all three. *Jen* (humaneness) is cognate with the homonymous *jen* (human [being]), and both are probably ultimately related to Proto-Indo-European *dhghem*, the root for "human," which means basically "earth." Compare Persian *zamīn* (earth, land), Russian *zemlya* (land), and Old Chinese *zim* ( = modern standard Mandarin *jen*). Hence, we may think of humans and *jen* as "earthlings," or those who spring from humus. The character for *jen* (humaneness) shows a man with the sign for "two," thus "[the way] a man [should relate to or treat] others." The usual translations for *jen* are "benevolence," "charity," "altruism," "kindness," and so forth. Although several of them are closely associated with certain historical, secular, and theological movements, I believe the use of some such terms as "humanism," "humanitarianism," "humaneness," or "humanity" as a rendering for *jen* is almost obligatory to show the intimate relationship of this Confucian ethical concept to *jen* (human [being]). The Confucian ideal of humanism and the Western tradition of Humanism share an emphasis on the achievements and concerns of mankind, but we may distinguish them by following the usual practice of capitalizing the latter. The other word for man or people in the *Tao Te Ching*, modern standard Mandarin *min*, is obviously cognate with English "man." Compare Indo-European *man* or *mon* and Old Chinese *myuhn*, Sanskrit *manu* (the thinking one, the creature with a mind), etc.

107

2.11—**right** The usual sinological translation of this term is "rectitude." Here and elsewhere it might well be interpreted as "correct governance," with which it is closely cognate in Sinitic languages.

4.1—**Reversal** Compare *Muṇḍaka Upaniṣad*, II.i.1, where all kinds of creatures are said to issue forth from the immutable (*brahman*) and return to it. Also see *Tao Te Ching*, 27.31, 60.3–4, 69.12, etc.

4.4—Compare this line with *Chāndogya Upaniṣad*, VI.ii.1.

5.5–6—I have left the technical terms yin and yang untranslated because they have already become a part of English vocabulary. While their significance in Chinese dualistic cosmology is known as the passive, female principle and the active, male principle, respectively, it may also be useful to understand these terms in their more primitive senses of shadeward and sunward, hence lunar and solar.

5.7—**vapors** Modern standard Mandarin *ch'i* (vital breath), for a discussion of which see the Afterword, pp. 137–138.

12.1—**mind** The Chinese word *hsin* means both "heart" and "mind."

13.19—This line bears a striking resemblance to the *Bhagavad Gītā*, II.23: "Weapons do not cut it."

14.18—**control** That is to say, it does not exercise dominion over them.

14.19—Almost identical to the last line of chapter 54.

15.9—**orifices of your heart** In ancient Chinese medicine, it was thought that the life breath (*ch'i*) flowed through the openings of the heart. It would seem that the author of the *Tao Te Ching* is grappling here with the problem of how to preserve one's vital energy. Because of the oddly arresting quality of the vocabulary here and in the parallel passage below (19.4–5), I have intentionally employed slightly obscure English phraseology.

15.10—Referring, presumably, to the senses. The same narrowing of consciousness is frequently described in very early Indian texts in almost exactly the same terms. See Feuerstein, p. 104. Compare *Kaṭha Upaniṣad*, II.ii.1; *Chāndogya Upaniṣad*, III.xiii.1–7, where the different types of vital breath that pass through these gates are outlined with precision; the *Bhagavad Gītā*, V.13, and especially VIII.12, which is quoted in the Afterword, pp. 144–145.

16.15—There is an obvious pun here between "bandit" (*tao*) and "the Way" (*Tao*). For similar reasons the thief is mentioned in the *Bhagavad Gītā*, III.12.

17.15—"This" signifies the Way. One knows the nature of all under heaven through observing things in accordance with the Way. Compare 65.17 and the note to 20.4.

18.11—**essence** The character may also quite literally be interpreted as "semen."

18.14–17—**implies, requires, is, entails** The Chinese text has the same word (modern standard Mandarin *yüeh*, "to say, call") for all of these English verbs.

19.4—**openings of his heart** Compare 15.9 above. The character as it appears here shows a heart inside of a gate. This is conventionally interpreted as meaning "depression" or "melancholy" (that is, the heart-mind closed up). From context, comparison with other manuscripts and early editions, and above all from the parallel passage cited at the beginning of this note, it is evident that this is not precisely what the author had in mind here. He intended, rather, to indicate the apertures of the heart.

19.4–6—See commentary to 15.9.

19.7—**the dust** The mundane world.

20.4—Neither of the two manuscripts from Ma-wang-tui answers this question, but the Fu I text has the concise rejoinder "Through this," implying the Way. Compare 17.15 and 65.17.

22.2, 4—**thrift** The author may have chosen the wrong word, but he wrote *se*, which means "stingy, mean, miserly, grasping." It sounds odd to have the Old Master advocating such behavior to one who would "rule men and serve heaven." He is not, however, advocating extreme parsimony or frugality here. Instead, he is advising the potential ruler to husband his own integrity. This becomes clear in lines 7ff.

23.3—**demons** Modern standard Mandarin *kuei*, often rendered as "ghost." A more exact translation might be "specters" or "lemures," as in ancient Roman religion.

25.8—**son of heaven** The emperor.

25.12—**to sit down** Presumably to meditate.

25.12—**this** The Way.

25.15—Compare Matt. 7:7 ("seek, and ye shall find") and 7:8 ("he that seeketh findeth"). These sayings of Jesus surely must be based on pre-Christian sentiments since we find them voiced in the *Tao Te Ching*, which originated at the other end of the continent.

25.16—Compare Apocrypha, Eccles. 2:1 ("the Lord . . . forgiveth sins").

26.3—Closely reminiscent of the *Bhagavad Gītā*, II.59.3.

26.5—Compare Saint Paul's injunction to "overcome evil with good" in Rom. 12:21.

30.9–10—Compare the quipu of various primitive societies.

32.4—Everywhere the word *hsiao* ([un]conventional) appears in this passage, it is meant to be a pun with the homophonous *hsiao* (small).

32.8—**three treasures** This expression is identical to the ancient Indian *triratna* or *ratnatraya*. Indeed, when Chinese Buddhists later translated these terms into their own language, they used the same two words (modern standard Mandarin *san-pao*) as here. In India, the notion of Three Jewels was common to various religious persuasions, each of which interpreted it in different ways. To the Buddhists it referred, of course, to the Buddha, the Dharma (his law or doctrine), and the Sangha (the Buddhist community). For the Jains, it signified *samyag-darśana* (correct perception or insight), *samyag-jñāna* (correct knowledge), and *samyag-cāritra* (correct conduct). The expression *ratnatraya* occurs in the titles of numerous Buddhist and Jain texts and even in those of some Vedānta and Śaivite (Hindu) treatises. It is not at all strange that the Taoists would take over this widespread ancient Indian expression and use it for their own purposes.

32.10—**compassion** Compare Sanskrit *karuṇa*, which the Chinese Buddhists subsequently translated with the same character as that used here by Lao Tzu.

34.2—**be host** Take the initiative.

34.14—**treasures** Compare line 32.8 and its note.

35.1–5—Compare the candid comments of Ssu-ma T'an, father of the great historian Ssu-ma Ch'ien (145–90? B.C.): "The Taoists propound 'non-action' which is also called 'non-inaction.' In reality, it is easy to practice but their words are hard to understand." See *Records of the Grand Historian* (K'ai-ming ed.), 130.279a.

35.8—**ignorance** Compare Sanskrit *ajñāna*, a key term in the *Bhagavad Gītā*.

38.15—**Heaven's net** This seems to be a veiled reference to *indrajāla* ("Indra's net"), mentioned several times already in the *Atharvaveda*. Compare also the net of Brahman in *Śvetāśvatara Upaniṣad*, V.3.

40.10—Many ancient Chinese rulers were almost fanatical in their pursuit of longevity. They resorted to all sorts of bizarre regimens and extravagant practices, including the ingestion of cinnabar (mercuric sulfide) which, of course, had the opposite effect on their life spans of what they desired, and the dispatching of innocent youths into the ocean to find the Isles of Immortality. It is ironic that Lao Tzu, the supposed author of this indictment against longevity (cf. also 33.8), would be made the emblem of life extension by many of his devotees. In truth, however, there are contradictory statements concerning the prolongation of life in *Tao Te Ching* (cf. 7.11, 13.12, 18.21, 41.9, 66.5, 74.22).

42.1—The bow is a favorite metaphor in early Indian texts. Compare *Muṇḍaka Upaniṣad*, II.ii.3–4.

42.15–17—Compare 46.18–21.

44.5—**contract** The imagery employed here is that of the system of tallies in ancient China whereby debtors were given the left-hand side of a piece of wood or bamboo that was split in half and creditors were given the right-hand side. When the latter wanted to collect from the former, they went with their side of the tally as proof of the loan and demanded payment.

45.1—Compare the title of the small book by Swami Ramdas: *The Pathless Path*.

45.2—Reminiscent of the famous Vedānta formula *neti neti* (not this, not that) indicating that Brahman is not designatable. See *Bṛhad-āraṇyaka Upaniṣad*, II.iii.6. Compare also the *Kena Upaniṣad*, I.5, where it is said that Brahman cannot be expressed in speech.

45.3–4—There would appear to be a contradiction between these two lines because "origin" and "mother" seem to mean the same thing. The editor(s) of the received text accordingly changed "myriad creatures" in the third line to "heaven and earth" in order to make it look like there was a difference in

111

content between the predicates of the two lines. Yet both of the Ma-wang-tui manuscripts clearly have "myriad creatures" in both of the lines. This powerfully confirms the very careful scholarship of Ma Hsü-lun and Chiang Hsi-ch'ang, who earlier in this century proved by referring to citations in Ssu-ma Ch'ien's "biography" of the Old Master, Wang Pi's commentary, the *Wen Tzu*, and to other sources that both lines should definitely read "myriad creatures." The real distinction between the two lines lies in the fact that the "nameless" refers to the Tao (the "origin") while the "named" signifies the fecund phenomenal universe ("mother") as it evolves after the primal beginning. Thus we see that although "origin" and "mother" are grammatically and syntactically parallel, they are not semantically identical.

46.13—**sage** The homophonous orthographical error here (the graph for "sound" is written instead of that for "sage"—both are pronounced *sheng* in modern standard Mandarin) may be telling. The percipient sage is one who is aware of the voices of the people. This reminds us of the Bodhisattva of Compassion, Avalokiteśvara (Kuan[-shih-]yin), whose name literally means "Perceiving the Sounds [of the World]."

48.1—Compare 8.3.

49.2, 4—**straw dogs** Used for sacrificial purposes, these were discarded indifferently at the conclusion of the ritual.

49.6—**bellows** The bellows (Sanskrit *bhastrikā*) is a basic form of *prāṇāyāma* (see Appendix, p. 160) going back at least to the *Yoga Upaniṣad* in which the vital breath is forcibly drawn in and out with a kind of pumping action.

49.9—The expression "hear much" in Chinese means "to be learned."

50—The best analysis of this short but very important chapter is by Conrady (1932).

50.6—**insubstantial** The manuscripts read simply "seem to exist."

51.3—**they do not live for themselves** Literally, "not self live," which could also mean "are not born of themselves" (self-generated).

53.1—See note to 42.1.

53.3—**temper** Literally, "to test [by running the finger over the edge of the blade]."

54.1—**While** The character that I have translated as "while" has caused so much consternation among translators and commentators that one famous modern scholar interpreted it as meaning "carrying [one's perplexed bodily soul] on one's head," and the renowned T'ang emperor, Hsüan-tsung, shifted it to the end of the previous chapter as a sort of exclamation point (!)! The majority of less daring scholars have simply pretended that it does not exist. Without here going into all of the painstaking philological proof that would be necessary to demonstrate it fully, the function of this particle standing at the head of the chapter is to serve as what may technically be called an initial aspectual auxiliary, or a particle for beginning a dependent clause.

54.2—**soul** The male and female / yang and yin / light and dark / spiritual and physical souls.

54.4—**Focus your vital breath** This phrase serves well as a translation of *prāṇāyāma* (see Appendix, p. 160).

54.6—**mirror** The heart. Ample justification for this interpretation may be found in the commentary of Ch'en Ku-ying (1984), p. 99 n. 6. See also the brilliant and learned article by Paul Demiéville on the spiritual mirror. Compare *Katha Upaniṣad*, II.iii.5.

54.7—**make it free of blemish** See the Afterword, p. 144.

54.9—**cunning** Literally "knowledge"; compare 28.5, 7. It is curious that "cunning" and "know[ing]" are cognate, both deriving from the Indo-European root *gno*. The equivalent Sinitic word (modern standard Mandarin *chih*) usually means "to know," but occasionally in the *Tao Te Ching* (see also 62.4) is better translated as "cunning."

54.10—**gate of heaven** There is a tremendous variety of opinion among the commentators over the signification of this expression. Some hold that it refers to the sense organs (ear, mouth, eyes, nose [cf. the note to 15.10 above]), others that it stands for the institutions of government, the processes of nature, the place where the soul goes in and comes out, the place in the Polar Star where the Lord of Heaven sits, a particular trigram of the *Book of Changes*, and so on. Still others see in this passage a sexual metaphor or a description of Taoist Yoga. In truth, several levels of interpretation are possible. The ambiguity may well have been intentional.

54.11—**Remain passive.** Literally, "can be female (bird)?"

113

54.15–17—Compare chapter 14.16–19, which ascribe the same attributes to the Way.

55.1—This celebrated metaphor of thirty spokes converging on a single hub was almost certainly inspired by the Indian fondness for using wheel images to demonstrate philosophical concepts. See, for example, *Śvetāśvatara Upaniṣad*, I.4; *Praśna Upaniṣad*, VI.6; *Muṇḍaka Upaniṣad*, II.ii.6; and especially *Praśna Upaniṣad*, II.6, which puts *prāṇa* at the center of the hub.

55.4—**pot** Compare *Chāndogya Upaniṣad*, VI.i.4.

56.1—**five** This chapter has three pentads (items listed in groups of five), but later Chinese authors elaborated many more. They are all ultimately based on the notion of Five Phases / Elements / Agents (water, fire, wood, metal, earth) that became popular in China about the same time as the *Tao Te Ching* was taking shape. It is noteworthy that the notion of Five Elements also occupies a prominent place in Indian metaphysics. Indeed, there were two sets (or, perhaps more accurately, two aspects) of the Five Elements in India, a greater and a lesser. The lesser are the five rudimentary, or subtle, elements (*pañca-tanmātrāṇi*): *śabda* (sound), *sparśa* (touch), *rūpa* (color), *rasa* (flavor), and *gandha* (smell). Three of these are represented in this chapter of *Tao Te Ching*. The greater are the five gross elements (*pañca-mahābhūtāni*): *pṛthivī* (earth), *ap* or *āpas* (water), *tejas* (fire), *vāyu* (wind), and *ākāśa* (ether). In rare Indian enumerations, the same Five [Gross] Elements occur as in the standard Chinese list (metal, wood, water, fire, earth). A similar conception existed in ancient Greek and Iranian philosophy and probably reflects an underlying pan-Eurasian system of thought.

56.1—**five colors** Sanskrit *pañca-varṇa* or *pañca-kāma-guṇā*. These are the five primary colors: *nīla* (blue), *pīta* (yellow), *lohita* (red), *avadāta* (white), and *kṛṣṇa* (black). They are the same as the five colors in China. Note that the Brahman wears over his shoulder a cord made up of threads of these five colors.

56.7—**five flavors** Salty, bitter, sour, acrid, sweet. Compare Sanskrit *pañca-rasa*.

56.9—**five tones** Traditional Chinese scales have five notes (*do, re, mi, sol, la*). Compare Sanskrit *pañca-tūrya*.

56.13—This formulation obliquely recalls our saying about a man's eyes (appetite) being bigger than his stomach (real needs). In other words, the sage understands human psychology with regard to desires.

114

57.1–2—These two enigmatic sayings have never before been interpreted in such a fashion that they both make some sense and fit with the following sentences. More literally, "favor is a disgrace comparable to being startled; honor is a great disaster comparable to the body." I suspect that these are very old sayings that were far from transparent even to the contemporaries of the *Tao Te Ching* author or compiler. That explains why he makes such an obvious effort (not altogether successful) in this chapter to explain them.

On the human body being an affliction, compare the following passage from the Buddhist text attributed to Nāgasena and entitled *Milindapañha [Questions of Menander]*, 73.24:

> The body, your majesty [Menander, an Indo-Greek king], has been likened to a wound by The Blessed One [the Buddha]; and, therefore, they who have retired from the world take care of their bodies as though they were wounds, without thereby becoming attached to them. And The Blessed One, your majesty, has spoken as follows:
>
> > "This monstrous wound hath outlets nine,
> > A damp, wet skin doth clothe it o'er;
> > At every point this unclean thing
> > Exudeth nasty, stinking smells."
>
> (Warren, p. 423)

57.6, 7—More literally, "To find it is, as it were, startling. / To lose it is, as it were, startling." This entire chapter is fraught with awkward scholarly explanations. The original core of the chapter probably consists solely of the first two lines. All of the rest is commentary, much of it quite pedestrian.

57.19—**then** More literally, "[in] such [a case] . . . ."

58.2, 4, 6—**"subtle," "rare," "serene"** The Chinese syllables for the three imperceptible qualities of the One enunciated at the beginning of this chapter all rhyme. Their order in later editions (including the Fu I text) of the *Tao Te Ching* is "serene," "rare," "subtle." The sounds of these syllables were approximately *yuh-hsyuh-wuh* in late Old Chinese. The *yuh-hsyuh-wuh* sequence led to the interesting (and provocative) speculation on the part of several distinguished nineteenth-century sinologists that Yahweh (Jehovah, the Tetragrammaton [YHWH] which seems to mean "the one who exists") or Īśvara (the self-existent divine power of Hinduism) may have been the ultimate inspiration for the triune Chinese epithet. In fact, *yuh-hsyuh-wuh* sounds more like Joshua (from a Hebrew expression meaning "the Lord is salvation") than it does like Yahweh. Be that as it may, the discovery of the

Ma-wang-tui texts, which have the sequence *wuh-hsyuh-yuh*, casts doubt on this particular attempt to link Chinese conceptions of Unity with notions of ineffable godhead elsewhere in Asia. Nonetheless, the question of how to account for the arrangement *yuh-hsyuh-wuh* in the received tradition remains. Furthermore, this is a typical Chinese method of analyzing polysyllabic foreign words: breaking what was originally a phonetic transcription into its component syllables and then assigning Chinese characters with superficially appropriate meanings to each of them. The same device has long been common in India as well for explicating technical terms. See *Chāndogya Upaniṣad*, I.iii.6–7; VIII.iii.5; *Advaya-tārakopaniṣad*, 16–17 (Ayyaṅgār, p. 8); and the well-known but wholly false etymologizing of the two syllables of *haṭha* (literally "violence" or "force") as "solar" and "lunar." Finally, the *Tao Te Ching* itself says unmistakably just below in line 9 of this chapter that the three qualities are bound together as one unit. For all of these and other reasons which must be omitted because they are even more complex, the three syllables for "subtle," "rare," and "serene" should be thought of as constituting a single word whose identity has not yet been firmly established.

59.21—**valley** The word "broad" has been added to the translation both for cadence and to reflect the implied meaning of the Chinese line.

60.1—I view the final particles of this and the next line as emphatics, not as copulatives. Literally, "arrive empty limit indeed" and "maintain stillness thorough indeed."

60.14—**ducal impartiality** The author is playing on the two meanings of *kung* ("duke" and "public, just, fair, equitable").

61.11—Literally, "We [are] self-so." The word for "self-so" in Chinese languages is *tzu-jan* (modern standard Mandarin pronunciation given). It is often translated as "nature." See the Afterword, p. 140, for additional information.

62.1—**Therefore** See the Afterword, pp. 123–124 and 152.

62.6.—**six family relationships** Those between father and son, elder and younger brother, husband and wife. These sentiments are exactly the opposite of Confucianism, which stressed that humaneness and righteousness, especially as applied to familial and other hierarchical relationships, were responsible for the preservation of the Way in society.

63.15–16—The last two lines of this chapter are attached to the beginning of the following chapter in the received text. Nonetheless, the rhyme scheme, the structure, the argument, and the wording all indicate that they belong here. If, however, we understand lines 1–4 of chapter 64 as an attack on pedantry (as Master Chuang seems to have done), it is conceivable that they should be placed ahead of them in that chapter. In any event, few of the chapter divisions in the received text of the *Tao Te Ching* have any validity (see pp. 151–152).

65.17—Compare the Upaniṣadic formula *etad vai tat* (this verily is that). Compare 25.12.

66.9–11—Compare 75.4–6.

68.13—There is a pun with "obtains" for "[awards] integrity," both of which have the same sound.

69.24–25—Literally, "The Way [takes as its] law [being] self-so." Compare note to 61.11.

70.4—Compare *Kaṭha Upaniṣad*, I.ii.21: "Sitting, he travels afar; lying, he goes everywhere." Compare *Tao Te Ching*, 10.8.

72.21—**infinity** Literally "limitless[ness]."

72.23—"Implements [of government]," in other words, "tools" or "subordinates."

72.27—The Chinese word for "carving" is a double pun in that the character used also means "to institute" and sounds like another word that means "to rule."

73.10—**puffed up** Compare the first line of chapter 66. "Shiveringly silent" is derived from a word whose most basic signification is "breath catches."

73.11—**meek** More literally, "may be filed down."

74.22—Compare the end of chapter 18.

75.4–6—Compare 66.9–11.

76.13—In dividing up the undifferentiated cosmos.

76.17–19—These lines offer but the barest glimpse of the magnificent parable recorded by Master Chuang at the beginning of his seventeenth chapter entitled "Autumn Waters" (*Master Chuang*). Compare 29.1–2. The image of many streams (individual entities) flowing into the ocean (*Brahman*) was a favorite of ancient Indian authors. See, for example, *Chāndogya Upaniṣad*, VI.x.1; *Bṛhad-āraṇyaka*, II.iv.11; IV.v.12; *Praśna Upaniṣad*, VI.5; *Muṇḍaka Upaniṣad*, III.ii.8; the *Bhagavad Gītā*, XI.28.1–2; and especially the *Bhagavad Gītā*, II.70 (Miller p. 38):

> As the mountainous depths
> of the ocean
> are unmoved when waters
> rush into it,
> so the man unmoved
> when desires enter him
> attains a peace that eludes
> the man of many desires.

77.8—**To die but not be forgotten** The received text reads this as "To die but not perish" where "perish" is homophonous and cognate with "forget" (still evident in modern standard Mandarin where both are pronounced *wang*). Here is a good example of the imposition of a religious interpretation on the *Tao Te Ching* that was not present in the original. Few commentators have questioned the absurdity and illogicality that result from the unwarranted emendation "He who dies but does not perish has longevity."

79.12–15—Compare 58.1, 3.

# AFTERWORD

## Part I:
### Did Lao Tzu Exist? The *Tao Te Ching* and Its Oral Background

There is universal acceptance among both scholars and devotees of the *Tao Te Ching* that its author was Lao Tzu (pronounced *lau dze* in modern standard Mandarin). This is a rather peculiar name for the presumed author of one of the most influential books ever written, for it means no more than "Old Master." Some have interpreted Lao Tzu as meaning "Old Boy" and have concocted weird tales of his having been born with a full head of white hair. However, there are so many precedents for Chinese thinkers being called master (*tzu*)—K'ung Tzu (Master K'ung, Confucius), Meng Tzu (Master Meng, Mencius), Mo Tzu (Master Mo, Mecius or Macius)—that there is little point in making other conjectures.

There is not a single shred of reliable biographical information concerning the identity of the Old Master. Despite frantic efforts to identify him with such shadowy figures as Lao P'eng, an archivist of the Chou dynasty, and others about whom next to nothing substantial other than their names is known, we simply do not know who Lao Tzu was, where or when he was born, what his occupation was, or anything else about him. All we have is a collection of sayings attributed to him that seems to have coalesced beginning sometime during the fourth century B.C. and was probably written down during the second half of the third century B.C.

There must have been a prototype for the Old Master. After all, someone did create a group of more or less coherent sayings that espouse a minimalist political strategy heavily laden with mystical overtones. Ultimately these sayings came to be written down in terse, codelike classical Chinese and were identified first as the book of the Old Master and much later as the *Tao Te Ching*.

But it is quite possible that more than one individual was responsible for formulating the sayings now attributed to the Old Master. Our philosopher may actually have been a composite personality. Many quotes attributed to an old master in books that predate the written versions of the *Tao Te Ching* do not appear in the latter text itself. Combined with other evidence that I will explore, this implies that the *Tao Te Ching* is a selection of proverbial wisdom from a larger body of sayings attributed to one or more old masters. However, because adherents of Taoist religion and philosophy think of the Old Master as an individual and since it would be awkward to make constant reference to "one or more old masters," I shall use the singular throughout this Afterword. This is by no means to recognize the historicity of a given old master as the sole author of the *Tao Te Ching* or even as the sole originator of these sayings.

If the *Tao Te Ching* was not the product of an identifiable author, then how do we explain its existence? The answer to this question is fairly straightforward: The *Tao Te Ching* is the result of a period of oral composition that lasted approximately three centuries (from circa 650–350 B.C.) During this period, it was common for philosophers to travel from state to state within the disintegrating Chinese empire, looking for a king who would put their ideas into practice. Initially their doctrines were formulated orally and transmitted in the same fashion from generation to generation among their followers. Finally, one of the adherents would take it upon himself to record the teachings of his master or school in short, pithy, classical Chinese statements. Still later, others might make additions or corrections. Thus the *Tao Te Ching* came about as a result of an editorial and commentarial process that is still going on today. But it was essentially completed by the end of the third century B.C. with some significant revisions and "improvements" some 500 years later.

Numerous vestiges of oral composition remain in the *Tao Te Ching* and fall into several different categories. One of the most striking features of the *Tao Te Ching* is that, in spite of its brevity, it includes a great deal of repetition. The reoccurrence of similar or identical passages might conceivably be the result of a conscious attempt to emphasize certain important doctrines, but textual analysis reveals that such repetitiousness is in fact endemic to oral recitations.

Sometimes the repetition is very close:

Diffuses the light,
Mingles with the dust,
Files away his sharp points,
Unravels his tangles.
(19.6–9)

files away sharp points,
unravels tangles,
diffuses light,
mingles with the dust.
(48.5–8)

At other times it is exact: "The Way is eternally nameless" (chapter 76, line 1 and chapter 81, line 1). Occasionally there is a replication of what is essentially the same metaphor, even when it is quite complicated:

Thirty spokes converge on a single hub,
    but it is in the space where there is nothing
      that the usefulness of the cart lies.
Clay is molded to make a pot,
    but it is in the space where there is nothing
      that the usefulness of the clay pot lies.
Cut out doors and windows to make a room,
    but it is in the spaces where there is nothing
      that the usefulness of the room lies.
(55.1–9)

Such modifications and variations are hallmarks of oral delivery, which relies upon them to assist the memory (additional instances of repetition are cited in the notes).

A detailed examination of the Ma-wang-tui silk manuscripts of the

*Tao Te Ching*—which date from around the beginning of the second century B.C.—shows that they are full of obvious writing errors. This is further indication that they had only recently evolved from an oral tradition. The scribes who copied them were often simply not certain of how to write a given utterance, and many of the errors reveal plainly that they were still very much influenced by the sounds of the words they were trying to record instead of just the meanings. By the third century A.D., with the establishment of the received text, all of the miswritings are "corrected." Unfortunately the "corrections" themselves are often wrong, causing much difficulty and confusion among later interpreters.

The *Tao Te Ching* is full of other examples that prove it to be a collection of proverbial wisdom which previously must have circulated orally. On the one hand we encounter completely isolated adages: "The soft and weak conquer the strong" (chapter 80, line 10). On the other hand we come across obvious quotations:

> There is a series of epigrams that say:
>     "The bright Way seems dim.
>     The forward Way seems backward.
>     The level Way seems bumpy. . . ."
>                     (3.10ff.)

In several instances, traces of editorial activity are obvious. Chapter 67, for example, consists of two very different types of material: proverbial adages and editorial comments. The chapter begins: "If it is bent, it will be preserved intact. . . ." Lines 28–29 of the same chapter identify this statement as an "old saying" and declare that it is quite true. It is not always easy to identify editorial comments in other chapters because they are seldom so clearly marked. Nonetheless, evidence of editorial tampering abounds. Most often, it is displayed in the jarring juxtaposition of dull explanation and poetic wisdom.

In addition, frequent statements of definition—such as "This is called . . ."—betray the heavy hand of an editor or compiler who is afraid his reader will not comprehend the message of the poetry he has gathered. It is difficult to imagine the Old Master himself making such clumsy remarks. Moreover, the inclusion of explanatory comment (for example, "What is the reason for this? It is because . . .") in the text is frequently obtrusive and can hardly be ascribed to a mystic or poet.

Further evidence of the oral origins of the *Tao Te Ching* is the use of mnemonic devices and formulaic language. They are relics of a stage when the sayings of the Old Master were handed down by word of mouth, rather than with brush and ink. Often the same grammatical pattern recurs over and over again in successive lines. Chain arguments are favored so that a whole series of propositions are linked together thus: if A then B, if B then C, if C . . . There is, in addition, extensive employment of parallel grammatical and syntactical structures. All of these devices helped people remember and retell the adages that were subsequently incorporated in the *Tao Te Ching*.

The Old Master is perhaps best represented in chapters such as 77, which consist entirely of a series of apothegms and maxims uncontaminated by any editorial insertions:

> Understanding others is knowledge,
> Understanding oneself is enlightenment;
> Conquering others is power,
> Conquering oneself is strength;
> Contentment is wealth;
> Forceful conduct is willfulness;
> Not losing one's rightful place is to endure,
> To die but not be forgotten is longevity.

A few chapters are carefully crafted and appear to be integral poetic sketches. Chapter 30, for example, is of deservedly high literary value. This chapter presents a simple, well-constructed picture of an imaginary primordial utopia with no discernible traces of oral composition. Chapters such as this were probably created expressly for the *Tao Te Ching* by the individual(s) responsible for the first written version(s) of the Old Master's sayings. Some chapters, however, barely cohere.

In order to understand better the matter of editorial intervention, let us look in greater depth at the mock conclusions that permeate the *Tao Te Ching*. Chapter 5, for example, contains two "conclusions" that follow one another in immediate succession. Both begin with "therefore," which implies a logical progression from what precedes. However, the first supposed conclusion does not seem to follow from the previous statements, and the second is even more fallacious. Chapter 62 even begins with the conclusional marker "therefore," although it is unrelated to the preceding chapter. All later editors simply removed the marker, but such omissions seriously distort the true composition of the text.

Another extreme example of a mock conclusion may be found in chapter 36 where the statement "Thus, he has no defects" serves no other purpose than to give the appearance of deductive argumentation. Indeed, more often than not, markers such as "therefore," "thus," and "for this reason" in the Tao Te Ching do not really serve to connect an argument with its conclusion.

How then do we explain their common occurrence at what seem to be crucial junctures? The answer lies in the very nature of the text itself. The first compilers of the scattered bits of proverbial wisdom attributed to the Old Master used these and other devices to give the appearance of a coherent text. They undoubtedly hoped to produce an integral text that could serve as the basis for the emerging school of Taoist thought. In fact, a critical reading of the Tao Te Ching— even in the Ma-wang-tui versions—reveals that it is burgeoning with non sequiturs, repetitions, and other obvious signs of homiletic derivation.

Dedicated readers of the Tao Te Ching—particularly after the founding of Taoist religious sects from the late second century A.D. on—have always assumed that the classic was constructed from start to finish by a single guiding intelligence. As a result they have tried to interpret it as they would any other closely reasoned philosophical discourse. The results—while displaying valiant determination to make sense of the book as a whole and of its constituent parts—are often sheer gibberish. The very frustration of the exegetes at not being able to make everything in the Tao Te Ching fit together snugly has only served to fuel further obscurity. For instance, no one is absolutely certain whether the following line should come at the end of chapter 63 or the beginning of chapter 64: "Abolish learning and you will be without worries." Nevertheless, partisans of both placements construct elaborate arguments defending their own preference. Indeed, a substantial measure of the fascination this small scripture has harbored for adherents of Taoism for more than two millennia stems from their inability to comprehend its overall structure.

It has been commonly thought that the Old Master lived from about 580–500 B.C. The main foundation for these dates is a pious legend of an encounter between him and Confucius, the founder of Confucianism, which was the orthodox system of Chinese thought until the first part of this century (naturally the Old Master comes out on top). Yet neither the Old Master nor his book is ever mentioned in the *Analects* of Confucius (551–479 B.C.). The same is true of the *Chronicle of Tso* (completed in 463 B.C. or later), which was a commentary on Confucius' *Spring and Autumn Annals*. Likewise we find no mention of the Old Master or his book in the work attributed to Mencius (372–289 B.C.), the second great Confucian sage. There is also no sign of the Old Master in the *Mecius (Master Mo)*, the canons of a noteworthy populist philosopher who lived (480–400? B.C.) between the times of Confucius and Mencius. We would expect that Master Chuang (355?–275? B.C.)—who was roughly contemporary with Mencius—might have mentioned a book by the Old Master should one have existed during his lifetime, since he is generally considered to have been a follower of the Way of the Old Master. Although he fails to do so, he does refer to the Old Master in the last chapter (33) of his book entitled "All Under Heaven," which is a survey of the major thinkers in China up to and including Master Chuang himself.

If the sayings of the Old Master had already been committed to writing by the time of Master Chuang, one would expect that he (or his successors) would have taken especial care to record their wording accurately. Yet in his exposition of the Old Master's thought, there is only one instance where Master Chuang comes close to quoting his presumed predecessor exactly (insofar as the Old Master is represented in the *Tao Te Ching*). All of Master Chuang's other quotations from the Old Master reflect well enough the general principles of his presumed guru but present his sayings in a jumbled fashion—again, if we take the *Tao Te Ching* as a standard. Virtually all other quotations purporting to come from the Old Master in sources that date from before the second half of the third century B.C. are similarly unreliable. Only in extremely rare cases do they tally exactly with his words as recorded in the *Tao Te Ching*, and in most cases they only vaguely approximate various parts of the classic. The situation improves drastically as we approach the second century B.C.

125

The sayings of the Old Master are first quoted or referred to in Warring States and Western Han period works such as *Master Chuang, Records of the Grand Historian,* and *Intrigues of the Warring States.* It therefore seems highly improbable that a work attributed to the Old Master could have been compiled before 476 B.C., the advent of the Warring States period. In terms of intellectual history, the Old Master represents a quietist reaction against the hierarchical, bureaucratic ideology of Confucius and his followers. The Old Master's digs at humaneness (*jen*), righteousness (*i*), etiquette (*li*), filial piety (*hsiao*), and so forth are plainly directed at the Confucian school. Such attacks most likely could not have come to pass before about the middle of the fourth century B.C., because until then Confucianism itself had not solidified sufficiently to be viewed as a threat to more spiritually minded individuals.

The composition of the *Master Chuang* book and other comparable works at the beginning of the third century may have provided the stimulus to assemble the wise sayings attributed to the Old Master during the course of the previous three centuries. The codification of the *Tao Te Ching* was probably essentially finished by the middle of the third century, and the first written exemplars must have appeared by about that time, setting the stage for the Ma-wang-tui silk manuscripts.

During the latter part of 1973, thirty silk manuscripts were excavated from a Han period tomb at Ma-wang-tui (literally "Horse King Mound") in the city of Changsha, Hunan province. They had been buried in the tomb of the son of Li Ts'ang, Marquis of Tai (a small southern feudal estate) and Prime Minister of Changsha. The son died in 168 B.C., so the manuscripts recovered from his tomb must date from before that time. Among them were two nearly complete texts of the *Tao Te Ching.* Based on the style of the calligraphy and other paleographical considerations, these texts have been dated to approximately the end of the third century and the beginning of the second century B.C. This means that they are roughly five centuries older than any previously available text of the *Tao Te Ching.*

The next stage in the evolution of the *Tao Te Ching* was the appearance around the beginning of the third century A.D. of the standard, or received, text, together with three notable commentaries upon it, the Hsiang-erh, the Wang Pi, and the Ho-shang Kung. Only the first half of the Hsiang-erh commentary survives. We know nothing of its author except that he leaned strongly in the direction of Yoga, a spiritual discipline emphasizing integration of mind and body. The oldest complete commentary is that of the brilliant Wang Pi (226–249) who died at the age of twenty-three. After it comes the Ho-shang Kung (translated as "Gentleman Who Lives by the River"), about whose author we are also totally in the dark. Where the Wang Pi commentary is more philosophical and metaphysical, the Ho-shang Kung commentary is more religious and emphasizes longevity.

Both commentaries bring their own agendas to the *Tao Te Ching* and, as a result, are not wholly reliable guides to the original text. Aside from minor details, the versions of the *Tao Te Ching* that they present are nearly identical and may be collectively referred to as the received text, although the Wang Pi version is favored by most scholars. Before the discovery of the Ma-wang-tui manuscripts, there were altogether half a dozen major versions of the text that date from before the ninth century A.D. Yet even when all six are consulted, a host of baffling questions remains.

It is only with the emergence of the Ma-wang-tui manuscripts that a substantial number of these problems can be solved. The chief reason for this is that they preserve many credible readings that later editors and commentators changed for their own political, polemical, or philosophical purposes, or simply because they could not comprehend them. The Ma-wang-tui manuscripts are not necessarily the primary text of the *Old Master*, but they do bring us much closer to it than any of the previously available versions.

Since the second century A.D., more than fifteen hundred commentaries have been devoted to the *Tao Te Ching*. Most of these commentaries do not significantly alter the received text itself, but there have been repeated attempts, even in this century, to remold the *Tao Te Ching* for one reason or another. Because ancient Chinese texts are difficult to read, the commentaries and subcommentaries attached to them can have a huge impact on a reader's understanding. A commentator might rearrange the chapters or parts to make the work as a whole seem more logical. Problematic characters might be replaced with more easily intelligible ones. When looking at the early commentaries, we must guard against their misleading or erroneous interpretations. These commentaries often give a false sense of security to the uncritical reader. We would do well to heed the words of the British sinologist Arthur Waley:

> All the commentaries, from Wang Pi's onwards down to the eighteenth century, are "scriptural"; that is to say that each commentator reinterprets the text according to his own particular tenets, without any intention or desire to discover what it meant originally. From my point of view they are therefore useless.
>
> From *The Way and Its Power* by Arthur Waley, p. 129.

By no means does this imply that the various commentaries have no value as records for the study of intellectual and religious history. Indeed, since 1949 it has even become possible to read the Old Master as espousing a materialist philosophy acceptable to Marxism! And there are numerous instances where the political and governmental concerns of the Ma-wang-tui manuscripts have been changed to meet more mystical and religious ends. In the early stages of the evolution of the *Tao Te Ching*, this sort of willful interpretation was commonplace.

The original *Tao Te Ching* is actually a very political book—otherwise, why so much attention to gaining all under heaven? Clearly, the aim of the author(s) was to show how to achieve hegemony over the empire. The sage who appears so often in the *Tao Te Ching* is the ideal ruler with the heart of a Yogin, an unlikely blend of India and China. The best way to control is through minimal interference and by keeping the people simple, without knowledge and without desires—two pervasive themes of the *Tao Te Ching*. As members of a modern, democratic society we may find reprehensible chapters such as 47, which advocate filling the bellies and emptying the minds of the people. But if we understand them as exemplifying a kind of third-century B.C. realpolitik, they begin to make sense as antidotes to the turbulent conditions that prevailed in society.

Although there is much in the *Tao Te Ching* of a mystical, metaphysical quality, the text as a whole is designed to serve as a handbook for the ruler. Perhaps this is the most intriguing aspect of the *Tao Te Ching* for a late-twentieth-century reader—the audacity of combining cosmic speculation and mundane governance in a single, slender tome. Some of the mundanity has been leached out of the received text by the religious preoccupations of those who were responsible for it, but in the Ma-wang-tui manuscripts it is still quite obvious.

Next to the Ma-wang-tui manuscripts the most important edition by far for anyone who strives to comprehend the *Tao Te Ching* as it existed during the late third century B.C. is that of Fu I (A.D. 555–640), which is usually referred to as the "ancient text" (*ku-pen*). It is based largely on a text of the *Tao Te Ching* said to have been found in the year 574 in the tomb of one of Hsiang Yü's concubines. Hsiang Yü was a renowned military and political personage at the end of the Chou dynasty who lived from 232–202 B.C. and was from the state of Ch'u. This is additional evidence that the *Tao Te Ching* probably first came to be written down during the latter part of the third century B.C. and in what were then considered to be the southern reaches of Chinese civilization. This puts the apparent source of the *Tao Te Ching* in a region that had access to Indian Yoga both by land and by sea, a factor that will receive due attention in the next two parts of the Afterword. It is also highly significant that Fu I's ancient text derives from the very same area as do the Ma-wang-tui manuscripts. It is possible that the Ma-wang-tui and Fu I texts were among the very first attempts to write down the *Tao Te Ching*.

While there are significant differences between the Ma-wang-tui and the received texts of the *Tao Te Ching*, they resemble each other to such a degree that we may conclude they are part of the same broad textual tradition. That is to say, they most likely constitute different versions of a single, parent work. Therefore, even the received text —when used judiciously—is of some value in our reading of the Ma-wang-tui manuscripts. Furthermore, certain studies of the *Tao Te Ching* carried out after the advent of "evidential learning" during the eighteenth century under the partial tutelage of the Jesuits and other Western scholars are occasionally useful in our efforts to understand the original *Tao Te Ching*. However, the solutions to most of the problems confronting the researcher can usually be found in the Ma-wang-tui manuscripts and the Fu I text together with other, contemporaneous materials.

Because of the discovery of the Ma-wang-tui manuscripts and the advancement of critical modern scholarship, specialists are currently in a better position to elucidate the original *Tao Te Ching* than at any time during the past two millennia and more. By closely analyzing the text and studying comparative religion, we now realize that oral composition played a significant role in the rise of the *Tao Te Ching*.

## Part II:
## The Meaning of the Title
## and Other Key Words

Now that we have become acquainted with the historical background of the *Tao Te Ching*, the most pressing task is to familiarize ourselves with the title and a few key terms. By exploring in depth the three words that make up the title and three other basic words that are intimately connected to the book, we will gain a more profound understanding of its overall import. Several additional concepts vital to the thought of the Old Master will also be introduced.

It may come as a bit of a shock to those who are fond of the *Tao Te Ching* to learn that, strictly speaking, the title is something of a misnomer. In the first place, the book was originally known simply as the *Old Master*, just as numerous other works of the Warring States period went by the names of the thinkers with whom they were most closely associated. The appellation "classic" only became attached to it during the succeeding Han period (206 B.C.–A.D. 220) by followers of Taoist religious sects. We can be fairly certain that orthodox Confucians would never have awarded it that honor.

*Tao Te Ching* or the *Way [and] Integrity Classic* is actually a plausible enough name for the book, except that the Ma-wang-tui manuscripts begin with the thirty-eighth chapter of the received text, which focuses on integrity, whereas the first chapter speaks of the Way; a more proper designation would actually be *Te Tao Ching* or *Integrity [and] Way Classic*. For the convenience of readers who are accustomed to the conventional title and to make it easier for those who might wish to consult previous scholarship on the classic, I have retained the wording *Tao Te Ching*.

The exact date on which the classic became known as the *Tao Te Ching* is unclear. Some scholars claim that this title was already used during the Western Han period (206 B.C.–A.D. 8), but all the sources they cite are actually from a much later time, even though they purport to draw on Han texts. According to his biography in the *History of* the *Chin Dynasty* (*Chin-shu*, written during the first half of the seventh century), the famous calligrapher Wang Hsi-chih (321–379) once copied out the *Tao Te Ching* in exchange for some fine geese that had been raised by a Taoist who lived in the mountains. This is probably the first explicit mention of the classic by this title. The next reliable occurrence of the title *Tao Te Ching* is in the "Bibliographical Treatise" (*Ching-chi Chih*) by Chang-sun Wu-chi (d. 659) et al., which is included in the *History of the Sui Dynasty*. This would seem to indicate that the classic was well known by its now customary title by no later than the Sui period (589–618).

The *Tao Te Ching* is also known popularly as the *Classic of Five Thousand Characters*, but the number five thousand is entirely whimsical. Extant versions actually range from 5,227 to 5,722 characters in length. The repeated attempts to prune the classic down to exactly five thousand characters are but another example of the impulse to shape the thinker and his book into a neat, preconceived package.

One of the most exciting recent developments in Chinese historical linguistics has a direct bearing on our investigation of the title. This is the discovery that there are unmistakable linkages between Old Chinese and Indo-European languages. Tsung-tung Chang, a Chinese scholar who has lived in Germany for three decades, recently published over two hundred proposed equivalences and is preparing a common lexicon for Old Chinese and Indo-European that will include more than fifteen hundred basic words. Since the work of Chang and others is still in its infancy, we do not yet know the exact nature of the relationship (that is, whether it is due to extensive borrowing, to some more fundamental kind of kinship, or a combination of the two). Nonetheless, investigators are heartened by the corroboration their work is receiving from archeology. It is now universally accepted, for example, that the chariots of the Shang dynasty burials in China from around 1200 B.C. are virtually identical with those of the Caucasus area between the Black and Caspian seas two centuries earlier.

Various distinctive metal implements (knives, axes, arrowheads, toggles, etc.) have been excavated from a continuum of easily traveled steppe land that runs all the way from northern China, through south Siberia, to northern Europe. Wherever goods are exchanged, so too are ideas and words. Thus, I feel fully justified in pointing out the Indo-European cognates to all of the key terms that will be discussed in the remainder of this part of the Afterword. I also believe that this analysis will serve to illuminate powerfully the meanings of these terms for readers as well as to demonstrate the nonexotic, nonperipheral quality of Chinese civilization. No longer may China be excluded from discussions of world history, for it has always been very much a part of the ebb and flow of human events and ideas. It is only our limited historiography that has underestimated China's place in the evolution of mankind.


## THE WAY/*Tao* (pronounced *dow*)

The central concept of the *Tao Te Ching*, of Taoist philosophy and religion, and indeed of all Chinese thought is Tao. The translation of Tao as "Way" is an easy matter. But our understanding of the term is heightened by a closer look at its early history, which shows that the Tao is deeply imbedded in elemental human experience. The archaic pronunciation of Tao sounded approximately like *drog* or *dorg*. This links it to the Proto-Indo-European root *drogh* (to run along) and Indo-European *dhorg* (way, movement). Related words in a few modern Indo-European languages are Russian *doroga* (way, road), Polish *droga* (way, road), Czech *draha* (way, track), Serbo-Croatian *draga* ([path through a] valley), and Norwegian dialect *drog* (trail of animals; valley). The latter two examples help to account for the frequent and memorable valley imagery of the *Tao Te Ching*; ways and valleys, it would appear, are bound together in our consciousness.

The nearest Sanskrit (Old Indian) cognates to Tao (*drog*) are *dhrajas* (course, motion) and *dhraj* (course). The most closely related English words are "track" and "trek," while "trail" and "tract" are derived from other cognate Indo-European roots. Following the Way, then, is like going on a cosmic trek. Even more unexpected than the panoply of Indo-European cognates for Tao (*drog*) is the Hebrew root *d-r-g* for the same word and Arabic *t-r-q*, which yields words meaning "track, path, way, way of doing things" and is important in Islamic philosophical discourse.

As a religious and philosophical concept, Tao is the all-pervading, self-existent, eternal cosmic unity, the source from which all created things emanate and to which they all return. This description could serve equally well for Brahman, the central principle of Indian philosophy and religion. Just as the Tao exists in the myriad creatures, so is Brahman present in all living beings. Brahman, like the Tao, is unborn or birthless (Sanskrit *aja;* modern standard Mandarin *wu-sheng*) and without beginning (*anādi; wu-shih*), both important ideas in *Master Chuang* and in later Taoism. *Wu-sheng*, in particular, becomes a standard epithet for the Mother Queen of the West, the main female deity in Taoism.

A frequent image in Indian religions is that of a way leading to unification with Brahman, that is, *Brahma-patha* (*patha* being cognate with "path"). The Buddhists translated this into Chinese as *Fan-tao*, literally "Brahman-Way," a striking expression that brings together these two manifestations of cosmic unity. Yoga, which I will have much to say about in Part III of the Afterword, is often thought of as a discipline that serves as a path to Brahman. In the *Bhagavad Gītā*, Krishna (who is an avatar of the godhead) repeatedly encourages the hero Arjuna to follow his way (*vartman*, also rendered as Tao in Buddhist Chinese). An even more common word for the Way in Indian religions is *mārga*. In Buddhism, for example, it was thought of as the means for escape from the misery of worldly existence. Among the many translations of *mārga* into Chinese were the following: *Tao, sheng-tao* (sagely way), *cheng-tao* (correct way), *sheng-tao* (way of victory), *chin-tao* (way of progress), and so forth. These and other usages make clear the correspondence of Tao to Indian religious concepts, including Brahman.

## INTEGRITY/*te* (pronounced *duh*)

The second word in the title of the *Tao Te Ching*, namely *te*, is far more difficult to handle than the first, as is evident from the astonishing sweep of thoughtful renderings of its meaning: power, action, life, inner potency, indarrectitude (inner uprightness), charisma, mana (impersonal supernatural force inherent in gods and sacred objects), sinderesis (conscience as the directive force of one's actions), and virtue, to name only a few of the brave attempts to convey the meaning of *te* in English. Of these, the last is by far the most frequently encountered. Unfortunately, it is also probably the least appropriate of all to serve as an accurate translation of *te* in the *Tao Te Ching*.

Much of the confusion surrounding the term *te* stems from its appropriation by Confucian moralists. Under their auspices it gradually came to mean "virtue" in the positive sense of innate goodness or the source of ethical behavior toward others. It did not connote the Latinate notion of "manliness, strength, capacity" (*virtūs*), which would be a more accurate translation of *te*. Regrettably, the English word "virtue" has taken the same moralistic path of evolution as that followed by modern standard Mandarin *te*.

To illustrate how far we have departed from the Old Master, *tao-te* has come to mean "morality," which is surely not what he had in mind by *tao* and *te*. To return to our exploration of the latter term alone, in the very first chapter of the Ma-wang-tui manuscripts, we encounter the expression *hsia-te*, which means "inferior *te*." Another common expression is *hsiung-te*, which signifies "malevolent *te*." If we were to render *te* as "virtue" in such instances, we would be faced with unwanted and unacceptable oxymorons. Clearly we must seek a more value-neutral term in modern English. I will begin this search by looking intently at the etymology of the Chinese word.

*Te* was pronounced approximately *dugh* during the early Chou period (about 1100 to 600 B.C.). The meanings it conveys in texts from that era are "character," "[good or bad] intentions," "quality," "disposition," "personality," "personhood," "personal strength," and "worth." There is a very close correlation between these meanings and words deriving from Proto-Indo-European *dhugh* (to be fit, of use, proper; acceptable; achieve). And there is a whole series of words derived from the related Teutonic verbal root *dugan*. These are Old High German *tugan*, Middle High German *tugen*, and modern German *taugen*, all of which mean "to be good, fit, of use." There is another cognate group of words relating to modern English "doughty" (meaning worthy, valiant, stouthearted) that also contribute to our understanding of *te*. They are Middle English *douhti*, *dohti*, or *dühti* (valiant), which goes back to late Old English *dohtig* and earlier Old English *dyhtig* (also "valiant").

As it is used in the *Tao Te Ching*, *te* signifies the personal qualities or strengths of the individual, one's personhood. *Te* is determined by the sum total of one's actions, good and bad. Therefore it is possible to speak of "cultivating one's *te*." Like karma, *te* is the moral weight of a person, which may be either positive or negative. In short, *te* is what you are. *Te* represents self-nature or self-realization, only in relation to the cosmos. It is in fact the actualization of the cosmic principle in the self. *Te* is the embodiment of the Way and is the character of all entities in the universe. Each creature, each object has a *te* which is its own manifestation of the Tao.

The relationship between individual *te* and cosmic Tao is almost exactly parallel with that between the Indian concept of *ātman* (soul) and Brahman (the all-pervading divine reality of the universe; literally "growth, expansion, swelling [of the spirit or soul]"). *Jīvātman* (the living soul) is the self, whereas *paramātman* (the utmost soul) is none other than Brahman: thus the quintessential Hindu formula *tat tvam asi* (that thou art). In other words, you are one with the universe. Tao and Brahman both represent cosmic unity, while *te* and *ātman* stand for the individual personality or character. Just as the *Bhagavad Gītā* portrays the absorption of the separate soul (*ātman*) into the cosmic Unity (Brahman), so the *Tao Te Ching* describes the assimilation of the individual personality (*te*) into the eternal Way (Tao).

The closest English approximation of *te* as used in the *Tao Te Ching* is "integrity." In simplest terms, integrity means no more than the wholeness or completeness of a given entity. Like *te*, it represents the selfhood of every being in the universe. Integrity may also have a moral dimension in the sense of adherence to a set of values. But it lacks the uniformly positive quality of the usual translation, "virtue," which subverts the moral ambiguity so important to our understanding of *te*.

## CLASSIC/*ching* (pronounced *jeang*)

*Ching* is the standard term in Chinese for "classic" or "scripture." However, its basic meaning is "warp of a fabric," and from this is derived the idea of "passing through," "experiencing," "transacting." *Ching* came to mean "classic" because it also signified the threads used to hold manuscripts together. Indeed, translators of Buddhist texts into Chinese used *ching* as an equivalent for Sanskrit *sūtra*, which is usually the final word in the titles of Buddhist scriptures. *Sūtra* literally means "thread" (compare English "suture") and probably derives from the root *siv* (defined by the cognate English word "to sew"), which also applies to the stitching that holds the leaves of a manuscript together. In addition, *sūtra* refers to compositions consisting of short sentences or aphoristic rules.

The Old Chinese sound of *ching* is roughly *gwing*. Without the final nasalization, this is very close to Proto-Indo-European *gwhi* (thread). Another form of the latter is *gwhi-slo*, which appears in Latin as *filum* (thread). English words ultimately derived from the Latin are "filament," "fillet," and "file" (in the sense of "line"). The latter may be traced back through Middle English *filen* and Middle French *filer*, which means "to string documents on a thread or wire" and is reminiscent of Chinese *ching* (book held together by thread). Other Indo-European cognates are Lithuanian *gysla* and Old Prussian *gislo*, both of which mean "vein," as well as Lithuanian *gija* (thread) and Welsh *gewyn* (sinew, nerve). Note that the latter, like Chinese *ching* (*gwing*), has a nasal ending. The character used for Chinese *ching* (*gwing*) almost certainly depicts the warp of a fabric on a loom.

Therefore, in strictly etymological terms, *Tao Te Ching* means "track-doughtiness-file." It would originally have been pronounced roughly as *drog-dugh-gwing*, had the title in its current form already existed during the Chou period. It is clear that all three words of the title *Tao Te Ching* are conceptually linked to Indian notions such as Brahman or *mārga*, karma or *ātman*, and *sūtra*. But etymologically they appear to be more closely related to European terms. It is thus conceivable that both China and India may have received the ideas these words represent from some such Europoids as the Tocharians or their predecessors who lived in central Asia before the formation of the *Tao Te Ching*. And China may have received these concepts more directly than did India. However, these are speculations that await the findings of archaeology for confirmation.

To complete our etymological journey, let us look briefly at several key terms from the body of the *Tao Te Ching* text.

## SAGE/*sheng-jen* (pronounced *shuhng-zren*)

This term, which occurs over thirty times in the text, represents the ideal Taoist ruler. There are a whole series of interesting parallels between Chinese *sheng* (Old Chinese *syang*, "sage") and English "sage." The first and most obvious is the similarity of their sounds. Still more striking is the fact that both of them are related to perceptiveness. The character used to write *sheng* (*syang*) shows this clearly by having an ear as its semantic classifier. The Proto-Indo-European root for "sage" is *sap-* (to taste, perceive). Several related English words are derived from this root (through Latin *sapere*—"to taste, have [good] taste, be sensible, wise"): sapid, sapient, sapor, savant, savor, savvy. "Sage" itself goes back to the same Latin word through Old French *sage*. *Jen* simply means "human" (see p. 107 for further discussion). Thus, *sheng-jen* means "sagacious person."


## VITAL BREATH/*ch'i* (pronounced *chee*)

While it only appears three times in the text, this term is key due to its role in the development of Taoist meditation techniques. These methods for calming the mind and prolonging life are described in the next part of the Afterword and in the Appendix.

The analogies between Chinese *ch'i* ("vital breath") and its Western and Indian equivalents are even more uncanny than in the case of *sheng-jen*. *Ch'i* refers to the metaphysical concept of material energy coursing through the body and the universe. The same concept exists in the Indian tradition as *prāṇa*, in the Greek tradition as *pneuma*, in the Latin tradition as *spiritus*, and in the Hebrew tradition as *ruaḥ*.

Moreover, there is evidence of a relationship between the Chinese word and certain Western terms. The archaic sound of *ch'i* is roughly *k'ied*, although the oldest Sinitic form of the word may have been something like *kvept*. There is little question about the early Chinese meaning of *ch'i* (*kvept*), because the pictograph used to represent it shows a few wisps of vapor rising. This calls to mind the Proto-Indo-European root *kwēp* (to smoke, to be emotionally agitated, etc.) and its derivatives. Most prominent among these derivatives is English "vapor" itself, which has lost the initial consonant and added an ending. Other Indo-European cognates are Lithuanian *kvẽpti* (to blow the breath), Lettish *kvēpt* (steam, smoke), Greek *kapnós* (smoke, vapor), and so forth. Most amazing is the cognate Sanskrit verb *kupyati* (he swells with rage, is angry), which literally means "he is smoking, steaming [mad]." This is precisely the same, very common idiomatic usage as in modern standard Mandarin *t'a sheng ch'i[-le]* (he is angry)—literally "he is generating vapors," the origin of which has long puzzled even native speakers.

## BEING, NONBEING/*yu, wu* (pronounced *yo, woo*)

This pair of terms literally means "there is" and "there is not." Together, these words constitute the ontological ground upon which the phenomenal world is played out. The Tao, ineffable and without attribute, is identified with nonbeing, yet it is the source of all creation, which is characterized as being. The Old Chinese pronunciation of *yu* was approximately *yex*. This seems to link it with English "is," which goes back to the Indo-European root *es* (to be). *Wu* is the same word with a negative prefix.

## NONACTION/*wu-wei* (pronounced *woo-weigh*)

If Tao and *te* are the most significant static or nounal concepts in the *Tao Te Ching*, *wu-wei* is certainly the most important dynamic or verbal notion set forth in the classic. Of all the Old Master's ideas, it is also the most difficult to grasp. *Wu-wei* does not imply absence of action. Rather, it indicates spontaneity and noninterference; that is, letting things follow their own natural course. For the ruler, this implies reliance on capable officials and the avoidance of an authoritarian posture. For the individual, it means accomplishing what is necessary without ulterior motive. Some commentators have explained *wu-wei* as connoting "nonpurposive" or "nonassertive" action. The Old Chinese pronunciation of *wei*, which means "to act as, be, make, do," was roughly *wjar*. This is quite likely related to "were" in English. *Wu* is simply the negative, which I have already discussed above.

## MYRIAD CREATURES/*wan-wu* (pronounced *wawn-woo*)

Literally "ten thousand objects," this expression refers to all things in the universe that have existence or being, in contrast to their origin —the Tao—which is without existence. The figure "ten thousand" signifies the vast variety of creatures and things in the world. It stands in opposition to the unity of the Tao from which they spring. The Old Chinese pronunciation of *wan-wu* was roughly *myanh-var*. This expression is clearly related to English "many varieties." The connection between *myanh* and "many" is obvious without having to cite earlier Indo-European antecedents. Still more striking is the affinity between Chinese *var* and the Indo-European root *var* of "variety," since both originally referred to the multicolored fur of animals (compare English "vair" and "miniver"). The earliest character used to write *wu* actually depicts a speckled bovine.

## UNHEWN LOG/*p'u* (pronounced *pooh*)

*P'u* (also translated as "uncarved block") is the most frequent metaphor in the *Tao Te Ching* for expressing the utter simplicity of the Way. Those who coined the phrase "Tao of Pooh" have captured a deeper truth than they may be aware of. The Old Chinese pronunciation of *p'u* was *phluk*. This is almost certainly related to the English word "block," which probably derives from the Indo-European root *bhelk* (beam).

## REVERSAL, RETURN, RENEWAL/*fan, kuei, fu* (pronounced *fawn, gway, foo*)

All of these terms suggest the continual return of the myriad creatures to the cosmic principle from which they arose. This is the "myth of the eternal return" so well analyzed by the great authority on comparative religion Mircea Eliade. The Old Chinese reconstruction of *kuei* is roughly *kwyed* and that of *fan* roughly *pran*. Since there are Sino-Tibetan roots for both (respectively *kwyerd* [turn in a circle] and *pran* [turn around]), we should not expect to find any immediate Indo-

European cognates. The Old Chinese reconstruction of *fu* (literally "go/come back") is roughly *byok*. A close cognate, written with the same character, may be tentatively reconstructed as *byog* and means "again." This reminds us of words such as *paky* (again) in Church Slavonic and *öfugr* (turned backward) in Old Norse that derive from Indo-European *apo*.

## NATURE/*tzu-jan* (pronounced *dze-zrawn*)

*Tzu-jan* literally means "self-so." This expression is also sometimes translated as "spontaneous." It implies that things are what they are by themselves; no agent causes them to be so. The Old Chinese reconstruction is approximately *sdyelv-lyan*, which resembles the old Germanic equivalent *selbh-lik* (self-like).

At the end of Part III and in the Appendix, I shall provide justification from the history of civilization for the wide-ranging approach to core Taoist terminology advocated here. But first we must examine more closely the rudiments of Taoist religion and thought. A good point of departure for this subject is the comparison of Taoism with the Hindu spiritual discipline known as Yoga ("union" or, more literally, "yoking [with godhead]"). We shall find that they agree in such varied aspects as the philosophies they espouse and the religious practices they advocate. Studying either is valuable for gaining an understanding of the other.

## Part III:
## Parallels Between Taoism and Yoga

From our examination of the oral background and of the title of the *Tao Te Ching*, we have already seen hints of Indian influence on its formation. In this part of the Afterword, I will provide evidence of a close relationship between the *Tao Te Ching* and the *Bhagavad Gītā*, widely considered to be the most important scripture of Hindu religion. Furthermore, as B. K. S. Iyengar and other experts hold, the basic philosophical premises of Yoga were given their first authoritative expression in the *Bhagavad Gītā*, just as Taoists regard the *Tao Te Ching* as the fountainhead of their tradition. Although a few earlier scholars have hinted at the possibility of a connection between Taoism and Yoga and between the *Bhagavad Gītā* and the *Tao Te Ching*, no one has been able to prove that they are actually related. I believe that the materials I present in this section, the Appendix, and the textual notes constitute convincing evidence that the obvious resemblances between the two traditions are not merely happenstance.

Since we are by now familiar with the rise of the *Tao Te Ching*, I will begin this section with a brief glimpse at the history of the *Bhagavad Gītā*. Unlike the *Tao Te Ching*, the *Bhagavad Gītā* has an explicit narrative context; it forms an essential part of *parvan* (book) VI of the great Indian epic *Mahābhārata*. This fact is also evident from its very title, which means "Song of the Lord [that is, Krishna]." The *Mahābhārata* (*Great Epic of the Bhārata Dynasty*) recounts events that took place between about 1400 and 800 B.C. The *Bhagavad Gītā* and the epic of which it is a part were probably written down sometime between about the fourth century B.C. and the second century A.D. Complicating their dating is the fact that both the epic and the *Bhagavad Gītā* must have undergone a long period of oral transmission before they were committed to writing. In any case, the core of the *Bhagavad Gītā* is probably at least one or two centuries older than the *Tao Te Ching*.

The *Bhagavad Gītā* consists of a very long dialogue between the warrior prince Arjuna and Krishna, a manifestation of the god Vishnu, who doubles as Arjuna's counselor and charioteer. This takes place on the battleground called Kurukṣetra (Field of the Kurus) as the war between the Pāndavas and the Kauravas, two ancient Indian clans, is about to commence. When the two armies draw up their ranks and face off, Arjuna becomes depressed at the thought of having to fight against many of his acquaintances and relatives who are in the opposing camp. He questions whether he should throw away his weapons and submit to a sure death or participate in a war that, no matter how just, is certain to result in much slaughter. Krishna reminds him that it is his duty to be a warrior and embarks upon a long discourse on action.

The chief lesson Krishna has to offer Arjuna is that altruistic or disinterested action (*niṣkāma karma*) leads to realization of Brahma. That is to say, one should act without regard or desire for the fruits (*phala*) of one's action. This idea is repeated over and over again in countless different formulations. These passages are of great importance for understanding the enigmatic concept of "nonaction" that is so prominent in the *Tao Te Ching*. "The person of superior integrity takes no action," says the Old Master, "nor has he a purpose for acting." We are told straightaway to "act through nonaction" and that "through nonaction, no action is left undone." In spite of the fact that this idea appears a dozen times and is obviously central to the Old Master's teachings, we can only vaguely surmise from the *Tao Te Ching* the specific implications of *wu-wei* (nonaction).

However, when we read the *Bhagavad Gītā*, we discover an exceedingly elaborate analysis of the nature and purpose of nonaction. The ideal of action without attachment is conveyed in many guises throughout the *Bhagavad Gītā*, for example, *akṛta* (nonaction), *akarma* (inaction), *naiṣkarmya* (freedom from action or actionlessness), *karmaṇām anārambhān* (noncommencement of action), and so forth. Krishna refers to himself as the "eternal nondoer" and states that the Yogin should think, "I do not do anything." He declares that he "sits indifferently unattached by these actions." Elsewhere, he condemns sitting and remembering. All of this reminds us of the "sitting and forgetting" advocated by the Taoists that later developed into a type of meditative practice.

If one acts in Brahman, he has abandoned attachment and will not be defiled by evil "any more than a lotus leaf by water," an eloquent image that subsequently became very popular in China. It is not actions themselves that are to be eschewed; it is only undue concern for their results ("fruits," in the language of the *Bhagavad Gītā*), which binds one to desires. Repeatedly, Krishna enjoins Arjuna to relinquish actions prompted by desire. There is a linkage between actions and desires in the *Tao Te Ching* as well, although it is not spelled out so explicitly.

Krishna makes clear his views on action and nonaction in the following passage:

> I desire no fruit of actions,
> and actions do not defile me;
> one who knows this about me
> is not bound by actions.

Knowing this, even ancient seekers
of freedom performed action—
do as these seers
did in ancient times.

What is action? What is inaction?
Even the poets were confused—
what I shall teach you of action
will free you from misfortune.

One should understand action,
understand wrong action,
and understand inaction too;
the way of action is obscure.

A man who sees inaction in action
and action in inaction
has understanding among men,
disciplined in all action he performs.

The wise say a man is learned
when his plans lack constructs of desire,
when his actions are burned
by the fire of knowledge.

Abandoning attachment to fruits
of action, always content, independent,
he does nothing at all
even when he engages in action.

He incurs no guilt if he has no hope,
restrains his thought and himself,
abandons possessions,
and performs actions with his body only.

Content with whatever comes by chance,
beyond dualities, free from envy,
impartial to failure and success,
he is not bound even when he acts.

       (IV.14–22, trans. Barbara Stoler Miller)

In the end, Krishna counsels Arjuna to rise above the dichotomy of
action and nonaction.

Aside from this striking fundamental resemblance between the *Tao Te Ching* and the *Bhagavad Gītā* with regard to nonaction, there are numerous other affinities between the two works. One is a shared concern for the relationship between the multitude, or aggregate, of created beings and the eternal cosmic principle that is their origin. Both focus on being and nonbeing. Both are preoccupied with the significance of wisdom, or knowledge, and nescience, or ignorance. Both texts strongly emphasize becoming free from desires and not prizing rare and costly goods. Both are concerned with birth, (long) life, and death. Like the *Bhagavad Gītā*, the *Tao Te Ching* openly discusses the purposes of war and the obligations of a soldier. Just a few of the key terms encountered in both texts are those for "return," "subtlety" (or "fineness"), "disorder," "affairs," "desire," "tranquility" (or "calm"), "taste," "supreme," "percipient sage," and "peace."

Entire stanzas of the *Bhagavad Gītā* read like miniature foreshadowings of the *Tao Te Ching*. In a burst of nominatives that would have warmed the heart of the Old Master when contemplating the Way, Krishna unfolds his all-encompassing nature:

Understanding, knowledge, nondelusion,
patience, truth, control, tranquility,
joy, suffering, being, nonbeing,
fear, and fearlessness . . .

Nonviolence, equanimity, contentment,
penance, charity, glory, disgrace,
these diverse attitudes
of creatures arise from me.

(X.4-5, Miller)

There are whole passages in the *Tao Te Ching* where the imagery and wording are very close to those of the *Bhagavad Gītā*. In book 3, stanza 38, of the *Bhagavad Gītā*, the obscuring of a mirror by dust as a metaphor for the clouding of the mind is almost identical to chapter 54, lines 6-7, of the *Tao Te Ching*. Even more startling is the likeness between book 8, stanza 12 of the *Bhagavad Gītā* and chapter 19, lines 4-5, of the *Tao Te Ching*: The former begins with "closing all the doors [of the body], shutting up the mind in the heart" and then goes on to direct the practitioner to channel his vital breath (*prāṇa*) up into his head to establish himself in Yogic concentration. The latter states that the practitioner "stopples the openings of his heart, closes his doors." Since these two lines are repeated verbatim in chapter 15, lines 9–10 of the *Tao Te Ching*, it appears as if they were taken over directly from Indian Yoga into Chinese Taoism. The manifestly Yogic content of the *Tao Te Ching* is also to be seen in the beginning of chapter 54, especially lines 4–5, which advise the practitioner to focus the breath until it is supremely soft.

By no means am I implying that the "author" of the *Tao Te Ching* sat down with a copy of the *Bhagavad Gītā* in hand and proceeded to translate it into Chinese. The fact that both texts evolved from oral traditions precludes such a simplistic scenario. Moreover, the sayings of the Old Master have a style and socioreligious character all their own. The *Tao Te Ching* was as much, if not far more, the product of internal sociopolitical conditions as it was the reaction to radically new religious and philosophical stimuli from without. As a result, it comes to very different conclusions from those of the *Bhagavad Gītā*. The Chinese classic emphasizes political skills and social harmony in preference to the theistic orientation of the Indian scripture. The *Bhagavad Gītā* is essentially a manual of spiritual discipline that has applications in the real world; the *Tao Te Ching* is basically a handbook for the ruler with mystical overtones. The *Bhagavad Gītā* advocates control of the mind and ultimate liberation; adherents of the *Tao Te Ching* espouse the indefinite protraction of the physical body.

Yet it remains that there are many remarkable correspondences between the *Bhagavad Gītā* and the *Tao Te Ching*. The most probable explanation is that the *Bhagavad Gītā* was transmitted to China in the same fashion that it was initially transmitted within India—by word of mouth. Particularly memorable images and powerful expressions would have been transferred virtually verbatim. In most instances, however, what the founders of Taoism absorbed from Yoga were radically new ideas concerning man and his place in the universe and a complementary physiological regimen (meditational discipline, dietary practices, flexing exercises, and so forth). Considering the immense linguistic, social, and philosophical differences between China and India, it is astounding that the kindredness of the *Bhagavad Gītā* and the *Tao Te Ching* shines through so conspicuously.

I must now address the sensitive issue of the precedence of Yoga versus that of Taoism. Given the complexities of the dating of the *Tao Te Ching* and the *Bhagavad Gītā*, if we rely strictly on these two sources alone, it is conceivable (though unlikely) that the Chinese classic might have influenced the Indian scripture. Certain distinctive aspects of Yoga that also show up in Taoism can be traced back to India beyond the first millennium B.C. and are systematically described over and over at great length (see the Appendix). However, in China they only begin to appear at the earliest around the middle of the first millennium B.C. And they are presented in a confused and cursory fashion until after the advent of Buddhism around the first century A.D. when they are reinforced by a new and more coherently conveyed wave of Indian influence. In short, if Indian Yoga did not exert a shaping force upon Chinese Taoism, the only other logical explanation is that both were molded by a third source. Since no such source is known, we can only assume an Indian priority and wait for additional data from future archaeological discoveries. However, it is improbable that new data would significantly alter our present understanding, because the case in favor of Indian priority is already massive (see the Appendix for a sampling of the evidence).

There are so many correspondences between Yoga and Taoism— even in the smallest and oddest details—throughout the history of their development that we might almost think of them as two variants of a single religious and philosophical system. Both conceive of conduits, tracts, channels, or arteries through which the vital breath, or energy, flows. They view the main channel as originating in the "root," or "tail," region of the body, then passing through the spinal column and flanked by two subsidiary channels. At death, the energized soul of both the Yogin and the Taoist emerges from the bregma (junction of the sagittal and coronal sutures at the top of the skull) to merge with the world-soul (Brahman, Tao). This is called the Way to Brahman by Yogis and the Marrow Way by Taoists.

Both Yoga and Taoism maintain that there are certain points in the body where energy is held, or bound, and that there are supports that guide the vital breath. Both envisage wheels or fields where this energy generates heat. Practitioners of both disciplines are said to possess an outer radiance that reflects a refined inner essence. In their esoteric forms, both are obsessed with semen retention (said to repair the brain)—not a preoccupation of religious practitioners that one

146

might expect to find springing up spontaneously in two such different cultures.

Yoga and Taoism also share a close association with internal and external alchemy. Both resort to the use of various charms, sacred syllables, and talismans as aids in meditation and for conveying secret knowledge. And both maintain that advanced accomplishment in their respective disciplines affords the practitioner special powers such as the ability to walk on water without sinking or on fire without getting burned. Claims of levitation have also been announced by those who style themselves Taoists and Yogins. These are only a few of the more obvious analogies between Taoism and Yoga.

By now, it is hoped that even the most hardened skeptic and the most ardent Chinese isolationist will admit that Yoga and Taoism bear such striking affinities to each other that they must be related in some fashion. But how do we account for this historically? It is commonly held that China was virtually cut off from the rest of humanity until about the middle of the second century B.C. This is simply wrong; fortunately archaeological discoveries and anthropological fieldwork are beginning to prove beyond the shadow of a doubt that, with rare exceptions, all of mankind—including China—has been continuously interacting across the face of the globe since the origin of the species.

It is also often claimed that China and India did not have any significant cultural intercourse until the first century A.D. This, too, is false, for there is now available artifactual evidence of Buddhism in China from no later than the middle of the first century B.C. China is mentioned by name, particularly as the source of silk, in a number of still earlier Indian texts. Trade between India and China, through a variety of overland and ocean routes, flourished well before the sayings of the Old Master came to be written down. As suggested earlier, whenever trade occurs between two countries, mutual cultural borrowing is inevitable.

The flow of Indian intellectual and spiritual influence into China that resulted in the rise of Taoism was undoubtedly mediated by a complex mix of peoples from western and central Asia. The same process was repeated later during the penetration of Buddhism into the heartland of China when Persian-speaking peoples, among others, played a crucial role in its transmission. Also, just as with Buddhism, Indian ideas instrumental in the rise of Taoism must have been brought to the south and central Chinese coast by trading ships that sometimes carried religious personages, paraphernalia, and scriptures.

In any event, Taoism (as well as other aspects of Chinese civilization) certainly did not materialize in a vacuum. As more thorough archaeological and anthropological studies are carried out on the periphery of China and as more unrestricted philological studies are undertaken on early Chinese texts, it becomes increasingly apparent that Chinese civilization is an integral part of the development of world civilization. Those who attempt to seal it off hermetically from the rest of mankind, for whatever purpose, not only distort Chinese history but fail to comprehend the true nature of human history outside of China.

The *Bhagavad Gītā* and the *Tao Te Ching* are not the only instances of Sino-Indian interaction in the development of Taoism. Master Chuang, Master Lieh, and other early Taoist thinkers also reveal distinct Indian philosophical and thematic proclivities at the same time as they are quintessentially Chinese. Taoist religion, too, shares much with Indian Buddhism. Its canon, ecclesiastical establishment, hierarchy of deities, ritual, and rules for communal living were all inspired by Indian models, and yet they have been assimilated in a way that makes them seem very much at home in China. Taoism, in turn, laid the foundations for the rise of perhaps the most genuinely Chinese of all Buddhist sects, Ch'an, which we know in its Japanese guise as Zen (both of which names are truncated transcriptions of Sanskrit *dhyāna* [meditation]). The circles and cycles of cultural interflow never cease.

## Part IV:
## Sinological Usages
## and Principles of Translation

The topics that need to be discussed in this section are somewhat technical. However, for the sinologist and for those who are curious about what sinologists do, the following observations are vital.

Since there are so many different systems available for spelling out Chinese languages, I must first say a few words about the crucial distinction between spoken language and written script so that I can explain my own choice. Ideally, the Chinese script is a device for recording on a surface the sentiments and sounds of the languages.

The script is definitely not equivalent to any of the spoken languages and, in many instances, there is an enormous gap between the two. We must be wary of using visual analysis of the ideographic and pictographic components of a character alone to arrive at the presumed meaning of the word from the spoken language it is meant to convey. The phonology of Chinese takes precedence over the script as it does with any language when one is trying to extract meaning. We also need to make a distinction between the various forms of extremely terse classical Chinese, which may never have been spoken, and the vernacular Sinitic languages, most of which have never been written down. The *Tao Te Ching*, naturally, is written in classical Chinese.

The transcription system used in this book is a slightly modified form of Wade-Giles romanization. Its chief competitor is Pinyin, which is the official romanization of the People's Republic of China and is used mainly by students whose work focuses on China during the second half of this century. I have picked Wade-Giles because it remains the sinological standard for the spelling of Mandarin and because nearly all libraries continue to use it for the cataloguing of Chinese authors, titles, and subjects. Furthermore, of the various competing systems, Wade-Giles is actually closer than most to scientific notations such as the International Phonetic Alphabet. Above all, the title of the classic is already widely known in the English-speaking world by its Wade-Giles transcription. Conversion to another romanization would render the title unrecognizable to many who are already familiar with it as the *Tao Te Ching*.

There are only two transcribed terms (yin and yang) in the entire text, and these have already been accepted into English. Thus there is no need to set forth here the whole Wade-Giles system, but it does behoove us at least to learn the correct pronunciation of the title and the name of the presumed author, Lao Tzu (see pp. 119, 133–134). *Tao* sounds exactly like Dow (as in Dow-Jones), *Te* is pronounced like Duh (as in "Duh, I dunno" but with a rising intonation), and *Ching* is almost the same as Jean with a -g sound stuck on at the end. Hence, *Tao Te Ching* might be phonetically transcribed for American speakers as *Dow Duh Jeang*. The Lao part of Lao Tzu sounds like "louse" minus the final sibilant. Tzu sounds not like "zoo," as many Americans tend to pronounce it, but rather like "adze" with the initial vowel missing.

As a matter of fact, neither the title *Tao Te Ching* nor the name Lao Tzu originally sounded the way we pronounce it now. The archaic reconstruction of the former is roughly *drog-dugh-gwing* and that of the latter is roughly *ruwh-tsyuh*. It is purely a sinological convention to cite ancient terms according to their modern standard Mandarin pronunciations. However, this is often quite misleading, since modern standard Mandarin is so far removed from the sounds of ancient Chinese languages that any resemblance between them is usually unrecognizable by all but those who are highly trained specialists. The problem is less severe for other modern Sinitic languages such as Cantonese, Taiwanese, and Shanghainese, which have preserved the ancient sounds to a much greater extent.

The dissonances between the realms of oral and written discourse in China pose enormous difficulties for the philologist, especially when he is dealing with a text like the *Tao Te Ching*, which had its origins in proverbial wisdom that first circulated orally and only came to be written down much later. During the transition from oral expression to written formulation in characters, a profound transformation occurred. What were once purely strings of sound possessed of rhythm, tone, accent, and pause that elicited in the mind of the auditor certain associated meanings became visual patterns spaced equidistantly on a flat surface that provided truncated semantic and phonetic clues to the thought of the author. Loquaciousness gave way to laconicism, affording great latitude to the imaginative interpreter.

The central role of imagination and intuition in the reading of classical Chinese accounts for the great diversity of opinion among the exegetes. It is for this reason that I have tried to reach beyond the commentators to the text of the *Tao Te Ching* and even, whenever possible, to get beyond the written text to the spoken language that inspired it. This may seem an impossible task to the novice, but there are rigorous linguistic methods that permit us to extrapolate from the terse written statements of the classics significant features of the oral formulations from which they were drawn. It is rather like the paleontologist's recreation of a Devonian amphibian on the basis of a few fossilized bones, or the forensic reconstruction of an entire skull on the basis of a molar, a bicuspid, a mandible, half a maxilla, one ethmoid, and a quarter of the occipital bone.

Unlike nearly all other sinological translators of the *Tao Te Ching*,

I place very little credence in the traditional commentators. More often than not, they simply lead one astray if one's objective is to understand the *Tao Te Ching* itself rather than the commentator's philosophical and religious programs. Because of a series of startling archaeological discoveries (oracle bones, bronze inscriptions, jade plaques, pottery marks, etc.) during the course of this century, we know far more today about the development of the Chinese script and Sinitic languages than did scholars at any time in the past. This is not to deny that there are items of value in the work of the early commentators, only to caution that they are often egregiously wrong because they were limited both by their sources and their methods. Most important of all, we are in possession of the Ma-wang-tui manuscripts, which are hundreds of years older and far more reliable than any previously known texts of the *Tao Te Ching*. Consequently, even though forty or fifty later editions sometimes agree on a certain reading, they may all be wrong simply because they did not have access to the early manuscripts.

The first principle of translation subscribed to herein is always to use the oldest available manuscript except when it is defective (that is, when it has lacunae, is torn, is illegible, etc.) or can be proven to be in error, in which case I rely on the next oldest text. When none of the early texts makes sense, I search for homophonous and near-homophonous cognates. Only when that fails to yield a reasonable reading do I suspect an orthographical error and begin to look for a character whose shape might have been mistaken for the one in question. My first assumption (borne out by many years of work on other ancient Chinese manuscripts) is that the author or scribe knew very well the sound of the word he wanted to record but was not always certain of the proper character that should be used to write it. I emend the text only as a last resort, which, fortunately, happens rarely in the present work.

This leads to the thorny matter of the chapters in the *Tao Te Ching* and whether or not they are legitimately applied to the Ma-wang-tui manuscripts, which are not marked consistently. I have numbered the chapters consecutively, according to the sequence they were found in the Ma-wang-tui manuscripts, while retaining in parentheses the conventional chapter divisions for easy reference for those already familiar with the *Tao Te Ching*. Readers will quickly notice that the order of the chapters in the Ma-wang-tui manuscripts is not the same as that

151

of the received text. For example, the Ma-wang-tui manuscripts begin with chapter 38 of the received text, chapter 40 is preceded by 41, chapters 80 and 81 (the final chapters of the received text) come before 67, and so forth.

While not fully punctuated, the older of the two Ma-wang-tui manuscripts occasionally has scribal marks that indicate where pauses should be made and stanzas separated. This is often helpful for understanding the text, and it contrasts with the vast majority of classical Chinese texts written before this century that consist solely of very long strings of characters spaced equidistantly. It should be noted that the breaks marked on the older of the two Ma-wang-tui manuscripts do not always coincide with the chapter divisions of the received text.

The division into eighty-one chapters has no validity whatsoever in terms of the original collection of the Old Master's sayings. Most of the chapters consist of two or more parts and are joined together for no particular reason other than the editors' desire to have a neat package. Conversely, in several cases, portions of the *Tao Te Ching* that are separated by chapter breaks in the received text might better be joined together. One chapter (62), for example, begins with a conclusion ("Therefore . . .").

It is futile to attempt to provide any rational basis for the division into eighty-one chapters since the number is purely arbitrary and has no organic bearing on the systematic ordering of the text. This particular number (*ekāśīti* in Sanskrit) was probably picked up from the Buddhists who favored it because it is the square of nine, which was itself fraught with all manner of symbolic significance for Indian mystics. One of the most hallowed Buddhist scriptures, the *Prajñāpāramitā-sūtra*, also had eighty-one divisions. Even in the few sporadic instances where chapter divisions are marked in the Ma-wang-tui manuscripts, they do not always coincide with those in the received text. Nonetheless, for purposes of comparison and analysis I have divided my translation into the customary eighty-one chapters.

As for annotations, there are two different approaches that might have been followed. On the one hand, there is the heavily annotated translation that so bristles with technical flourishes as to scare away all nonsinologists. On the other hand, there is the translation that is totally devoid of commentary and that often leaves the lay reader guessing and wondering at every turn. I have tried to strike a happy balance between these two extremes by providing notes that would satisfy the curiosity or puzzlement of the beginner and the legitimate needs of the sinologist, but they appear at the back of the book so as not to clutter up the pages of the translation. For the same reason, the Notes are keyed to the text by line and word rather than by superscript numbers. In general, my aim has been to make the translation completely integral and self-explanatory. Thus, there should be no need to consult the Notes or the Afterword upon a first reading of the *Tao Te Ching* itself. The Notes and the Afterword are intended for those who reread the text and require additional commentary in the course of their deeper analysis and reflection.

My chief goal in undertaking this translation has been to create a thoroughly new English version of the *Tao Te Ching*. During its preparation, I intentionally avoided consulting other translations so that I would not be influenced by them. Aside from not wanting to be repetitive and stale, I did not wish to be trapped by facile solutions bequeathed by the received text, its editors, commentators, and translators. As a tribute to the unexpected re-emergence of the Ma-wang-tui manuscripts, I have endeavored to provide a fresh examination on their own terms, one not burdened by two millennia of religious and philosophical exegesis. If others wish to amalgamate the Ma-wang-tui manuscripts with the received text, that is their prerogative, but it is not what I have set out to do here. For those who are interested in learning about later interpretations of the *Tao Te Ching*, several previous translations that include extensive commentaries and explanations are listed in the bibliography.

# APPENDIX

This Appendix is designed for those who want additional information on the relationship between Yoga and Taoism.

In his landmark comparative study *Sufism and Taoism*, Toshihiko Izutsu discerns what he calls "the two pivots of a world-view," namely "the Absolute and the Perfect Man." Izutsu sees these twin pivots (Tao and *te*, as it were) developing independently in different places and ages. Nonetheless, it would be difficult to prove that Sufism and Taoism were absolutely unrelated. This is especially the case when we consider that both Persia and China had commercial, cultural, and political ties with each other and with India during the period when Sufism developed. Similarly, given the unmistakable resemblances between Taoism and Yoga, it would be virtually impossible to prove that they have no historical connections whatsoever. Even Joseph Needham (pp. 257–88), the great advocate of the autonomy of Chinese technology, is persuaded by the evidence to admit that there must have been some sort of influence operating between these two systems of thought. The difficulty is in trying to sort out which came first.

Because the question of priority is too complicated to include in the main body of the Afterword, I have gathered in this Appendix some of the more pertinent material. The first item of evidence from the Chinese side is an isolated inscription on ten pieces of jade making up a small knob that is datable to approximately the year 380 B.C.:

155

In moving the vital breath (*hsing ch'i*) [through the body, hold it deep and] thereby accumulate it. Having accumulated it, let it extend (*shen*). When it extends, it goes downward. After it goes downward, it settles. Once it is settled, it becomes firm. Having become firm, it sprouts [compare Yogic *bīja* ("seed" or "germ")]. After it sprouts, it grows. Once grown, then it withdraws. Having withdrawn, it becomes celestial [that is, yang]. The celestial potency presses upward, the terrestrial potency presses downward. [He who] follows along [with this natural propensity of the vital breath] lives; [he who] goes against it dies.

(Kuo Mo-jo, p. 9)

Without addressing the choppy, convoluted style in which it is written, I need only point out that every essential element of this inscription can be traced to Indian texts that date from 900 to 200 B.C. Among these are the thirteen classical *Upaniṣads* (c. 700–300 B.C.), which are supplementary teachings attached to the *Vedas*, India's most ancient body of knowledge. For example, the *Maitrī Upaniṣad* offers an elaborate exposition of the five types of breath (*prāṇa, apāna, samāna, udāna, vyāna*), their movement upward and downward and throughout each limb, as well as their relationship to life and death. The whole second *khaṇḍa* (section) of the *Muṇḍaka Upaniṣad* has so many close parallels to the *Tao Te Ching* that it deserves the most thorough study by serious students of the Taoist classic. Here I shall cite only a part of the sixth stanza, which bears obvious resemblance to one of the most celebrated images of the Old Master:

Where the channels (*nāḍi*) come together
Like spokes in the hub of a wheel,
Therein he (imperishable Brahman as manifested
    in the individual soul [*ātman*]) moves about
Becoming manifold.

The corresponding passage from the *Tao Te Ching* (chapter 55, lines 1–3) has a slightly different application, but the common inspiration is evident:

Thirty spokes converge on a single hub,
    but it is in the space where there is nothing
    that the usefulness of the cart lies.

156

In one of the earliest *Upaniṣads*, the *Chāndogya*, we find an exposition of the microcosmology of the human body that certainly prefigures Taoist notions of a much later period:

> A hundred and one are the arteries (*nāḍi*) of the heart,
> One of them leads up to the crown of the head;
> Going upward through that, one becomes immortal (*amṛta*),
> The others serve for going in various directions. . . .
>
> (translation adapted from Radhakrishnan, p. 501)

This is not just an isolated occurrence, for the same conception is restated in the *Kaṭha Upaniṣad*, the *Taittirīya Upaniṣad*, and the *Praśna Upaniṣad*.

Yogic concentration of all the senses upon the self is clearly evident in the *Chāndogya Upaniṣad*. In the *Maitrī Upaniṣad*, Yoga is mentioned specifically by name and defined in a manner that would fit Taoism almost as well:

> The oneness of the breath, the mind, and likewise of the senses,
> The abandonment of all conditions of existence, this is designated Yoga.
>
> (translation adapted from Radhakrishnan, p. 835)

By the time of the *Yoga Sūtras* and *Yoga Upaniṣads* (the earliest layers of which date to no later than the second century B.C.), the complete pre–Tantric Yogic system had received explicit and elaborate codification in written form. Patañjali, who wrote the first three books of the *Yoga Sūtras* around the second century B.C., recognizes (I.1) that he was not the creator of Yogic techniques but only wanted to present them in a rigorously systematic fashion. Those who take the trouble to read attentively the early Indian texts just cited, particularly the classical *Upaniṣads*, will realize that they foreshadow the entire philosophical, religious, and physiological foundations of Taoism, but not its social and political components, which are distinctively Chinese.

Still farther back in time, the *Atharva Veda* (900 B.C. or before) has a very long chapter dealing exclusively with the vital breath and its circulation (to mention only one aspect that is pertinent to Taoism). Although the entire chapter deserves quotation and careful exami-

nation by all conscientious students of Taoism, I have space to present
only nine stanzas here:

> When breath with thunder roars at the plants, they are fertilized, they
> receive the germ, consequently they are born abundantly.
>
> Rained upon, the plants spoke with breath (saying): You have ex-
> tended our life, you have made us all fragrant.
>
> Homage, breath, be to you breathing up, homage to you breathing
> down; homage to you turning away, homage to you turning hither;
> here is homage to all of you.
>
> Your dear form, breath, and your even dearer form, also the healing
> power that is yours, of that put in us, that we may live.
>
> Breath is the shining One (the Queen), breath the Directress, all
> revere breath; breath is the sun and the moon, breath they say is the
> Lord of Creatures.
>
> Man, while still in the womb, functions with nether and upper breath
> [compare the "womb breathing" of the Taoists]; when you, breath,
> quicken him, then he is born again.
>
> When breath has rained with rain upon the great earth, plants are
> generated, and all herbs that exist.
>
> Who is lord over this (all) of every source, over all that moves, whose
> bow is swift among (against?) the unwearied ones,—O breath, homage
> be to thee.
>
> O breath, turn not away from me; you shall be no other than myself.
> I bind you to myself, breath, like the child of the waters, that I may
> live.
>
> (XI.iv.3, 6, 8–9, 12, 14, 17, 23, 26; trans. Edgerton)

If there were still any doubts about the vast antiquity of Yogic
physiological discipline in comparison with similar Taoist practices,
one need only recall that *āsana* (postures) have been found represented
on seals and statuettes from Mohenjo Daro and Harappā, sites of the
Indus Valley civilization that date back to about 2500 B.C. Although
we cannot be certain that the individuals so depicted are actually
engaged in meditation (*dhyāna*), it is noteworthy that some elements
of Yoga, as Eliade has asserted, must have preceded the arrival of the

Aryans in the south Asian subcontinent. Yoga is reflected as well in many ancient archaeological monuments of India, Indochina, and Indonesia (see Pott). Specific meditational postures are already mentioned by name in the Indian epic *Mahābhārata* of which the *Bhagavad Gītā* forms a part. These include the *maṇḍūkayoga* (frog yoga) and *vīrāsana* (posture of a hero).

The next piece of evidence from the Chinese side is quite well known and has been cited by most competent authorities as providing crucial data for the origins of Taoist physical exercises. It comes from one of the later chapters of the *Master Chuang* and may be dated roughly to 250 B.C., just about the time when the *Tao Te Ching* came to be written down:

> Blowing and breathing, exhaling and inhaling, expelling the old and taking in the new, bear strides and bird stretches—[these activities are designed] to achieve longevity and that is all. They are favored by those who [through] channeling [of the vital breath] and flexions [of the muscles and the joints wish to emulate] the longevity of Methuselah.
>
> (*Concordance to Chuang Tzu*, ch. 15, p. 40)

The odd expression "bear strides" is illustrated on another recently unearthed document from Ma-wang-tui. A silk manuscript from the same Han tomb that yielded the manuscripts of the *Tao Te Ching* consists of painted designs of gymnastic exercises that date to 168 B.C. or before. Originally, the manuscript showed over forty exercises, but only twenty-eight survive intact in its present fragmentary condition.

One striking feature of the twenty-eight exercises depicted on the fragmentary silk manuscript is that many of them are named after birds and animals (wolf, kite, sparrow hawk, ape, crane, and so on). This immediately reminds us of Yogic *āsana* (postures) that are patterned after the movements or poses of similar (and sometimes even identical) creatures: eagle, swan, peacock, crane, heron, cock, pigeon, partridge, tortoise, fish, monkey, lion, camel, frog, horse, cow, dog, crocodile, snake, locust, scorpion, and so on. One might say it is natural for man to imitate animals when devising physical exercises, but there are other grounds for believing that Taoist gymnastics and Yogic postures have a common origin.

159

Let us discuss the native designations for this type of exercise in India and in China. The Chinese word is the bisyllabic *tao-yin*, which means leading, guiding, channeling, or duction (an obsolete English term that we may revive for this purpose) and basically signifies the directed movement through the body of *ch'i* (vital breath) as well as the controlled extension or drawing out of the limbs, muscles, and joints of the body. This sounds suspiciously close to Yogic breath control (*prāṇāyāma*, from *prāṇa* [vital breath] and *āyāma* [lengthening, extension]). *Prāṇāyāma* is the rhythmically restrained drawing in and out of the breath.

To return to our discussion of the passage from *Master Chuang*, after "bear strides" comes "bird stretches." While not among the surviving postures and labels on the silk manuscript from Ma-wang-tui, it clearly echoes several Indian *āsana*. The next phrases show that Master Chuang disparages the pursuit of physical longevity, perhaps a sly dig at the Old Master and his ilk. At least one strand of the *Tao Te Ching* itself, however, is definitely opposed to conscientious life extension and breath control (see chapter 18, lines 16–17; chapter 40, lines 9–15 and the note to line 10; and chapter 77, line 8).

I have cited above many early Indian texts that outline Yoga philosophy, yet they can only have constituted but a small fraction of what was transmitted orally in fuller form. Hence it is not possible in every case to provide specific textual references for the sources of Indian influence on the development of Taoism. For example, it would be difficult to pinpoint a single Indian source for the microcosmic physiological conception of the human body so characteristic of Taoism, yet we know that it was already securely in place in India long before being elaborated in China. So pervasive was the Indian impact upon the growth of Taoist metaphysics that the latter—especially in its formative stages—is not wholly intelligible without consulting its Yogic background. Our appreciation of Chinese thought in general is enhanced by the recognition that, in fact, it is intimately connected to world philosophy.

The rise of Taoism is not just a matter of Sino-Indian cultural relations. A tremendous intellectual ferment convulsed all of Eurasia around the middle of the first millennium B.C. Within a brief span of approximately a century, the following major systems of thought were articulated or adumbrated: pre-Socratic Greek philosophy (Thales and

Anaximander of Miletus), Confucianism, Mohism, Upaniṣadic Hinduism, Jainism, Taoism, Buddhism, Zoroastrianism, and Biblical Judaism. It is highly unlikely that these great movements were utterly independent phenomena (see Benjamin Schwartz's comments on the Axial Age in his *The World of Thought in Ancient China*, pp. 2–3). Indeed, they were probably closely tied to the explosive growth in the use of iron during the preceding two centuries, which caused tremendous social and political rearrangements (see Calder, p. 169).

The political manifestation of the widespread use of iron in China was the breakup of the feudal Chou empire into seven main and many lesser states about 475 B.C. After more than 250 years of prolonged fighting, the state of Ch'in emerged as the leading power to reunite China in 221 B.C. It is significant both that the original Ch'in base was far to the northwest and that her soldiers were well equipped with iron and advanced metallic alloy weapons. The procurement of these new technologies enabled the Ch'in armies to defeat the other warring states farther east that had splintered off from the Chou dynasty. The consolidation of the Chinese state under the First Emperor (Shih-huang) of the Ch'in probably thus represents the last eastward wave of the conquests of Darius the Great of Persia (558?–486 B.C.) and Alexander the Great of Macedonia (356–323 B.C.). This interpretation has been forcefully corroborated by the recent discovery in Sinkiang ("New Borders"—the Chinese-controlled part of central Asia) of a large copper statue of a west Asiatic warrior that is preserved in the regional museum at Urumchi. He dates to approximately the fourth century B.C. and is depicted in a kneeling posture almost identical to that of many infantrymen in the terra cotta army of the First Emperor of the Ch'in. The existence of a large Roman military encampment even farther east in Kansu province during the first century B.C. has also recently been documented. It was through these soldiers that the transfer of iron technology and the ideas that came in its wake were achieved.

**Note:** Scholars who wish to obtain complete documentation for all points raised in the Afterword and who desire fuller annotations for the text may write to the author for a separate, sinologically oriented publication concerning the *Tao Te Ching*.

# SELECTED
# BIBLIOGRAPHY

Ames, Roger T. *The Art of Rulership: A Study in Ancient Chinese Political Thought.* Honolulu: University of Hawaii Press, 1983.

Ayyaṅgār, T. R. Śrīnivāsa, trans. *The Yoga-Upaniṣad-s.* Edited by Paṇḍit S. Subrahmaṇya Śāstrī. Madras: The Adyar Library, 1938.

Boltz, William G. "The *Lao tzu* Text that Wang Pi and Ho-shang Kung Never Saw." *Bulletin of the School of Oriental and African Studies* 48, no. 3 (1985):493–501.

————. "The Religious and Philosophical Significance of the 'Hsiang erh' *Lao tzu* in the Light of the Ma-wang-tui Silk Manuscripts." *Bulletin of the School of Oriental and African Studies* 45, no. 1 (1982):95–117.

————. "Textual Criticism and the Ma-wang-tui *Lao tzu*." *Harvard Journal of Asiatic Studies* 44, no. 1 (June 1984):185–224.

Calder, Nigel. *Timescale: An Atlas of the Fourth Dimension.* New York: Viking, 1983.

Chan, Wing-tsit, trans. and annot. *The Way of Lao Tzu (Tao-te ching).* Indianapolis: Bobbs-Merrill, 1963.

Chang, Tsung-tung. "Indo-European Vocabulary in Old Chinese: A New Thesis on the Emergence of Chinese Language and Civilization in the Late Neolithic Age." *Sino-Platonic Papers* 7 (January 1988), 56 pages.

Chatterji, Suniti Kumar. "India and China: Ancient Contacts—What India Received from China." *Journal of the Asiatic Society* [Calcutta] 1, no. 1 (1959):89–122.

Chen, Ellen M. *The Tao Te Ching: A New Translation with Commentary.* New York: Paragon, 1989.

Ch'en Ku-ying. *Lao Tzu Chu I chi P'ing-chieh* [Lao Tzu: Commentary, translation, and critique]. Peking: Chung-hua Shu-chü, 1984.

————. *Lao Tzu: Text, Notes, and Comments.* Translated by Rhett Y. W. Young and Roger T. Ames. San Francisco: Chinese Materials Center, 1977.

Ch'en Yin-k'o. "*San-kuo Chih* Ts'ao Ch'ung Hua-t'o Chuan yü Fo-chiao Kushih [Buddhist Tales and the Biographies of Ts'ao Ch'ung and Hua-t'o in the *History of the Three Kingdoms*]." In *Ch'en Yin-k'o Hsien-sheng Lun-wen Chi* [Collected works of Ch'en Yin-k'o], pp. 417–20. Vol. 2. Taipei: San-jenhsing Ch'u-pan-she, 1974.

Chiang Hsi-ch'ang. *Lao Tzu Chiao-ku* [Lao Tzu: Collation and commentary]. Shanghai: Commercial Press, 1937.

Conrady, A. "Indischer Einfluss in China im 4-Jahrhundert v. Chr." *Zeitschrift der Deutscher Morgenländischen Gesellschaft* 60 (1906):335–51.

————. "Zu Lao-Tze, cap. 6." *Asia Major* 7 (1932):150–56.

DeFrancis, John. *The Chinese Language: Fact and Fantasy.* Honolulu: University of Hawaii Press, 1984.

————. *Visible Speech: The Diverse Oneness of Writing Systems.* Honolulu: University of Hawaii Press, 1989.

Demiéville, Paul. "Le miroir spirituel." *Sinologica* 1, no. 2 (1947):112–37.

Duyvendak, J. J. L., trans. and annot. *Tao Te Ching: The Book of the Way and Its Virtue.* The Wisdom of the East Series. London: John Murray, 1954.

Edgerton, Franklin, trans., intro., and notes. *The Beginnings of Indian Philosophy: Selections from the Rig Veda, Atharva Veda, Upaniṣads, and Mahābhārata.* Cambridge, Mass.: Harvard University Press, 1965.

Eliade, Mircea. *The Myth of the Eternal Return*, trans. from the French by Willard R. Trask. Bollingen Series, 46. New York: Pantheon, 1954.

————. *Yoga: Immortality and Freedom*, trans. from the French by Willard R. Trask. Bollingen Series, 56. 2d ed. Princeton: Princeton University Press, 1970.

*Encyclopaedia Britannica*, fifteenth ed., s.v. "Taoism," "Taoism, history of," and "Taoist literature."

Erkes, Eduard. *Ho-shang-kung's Commentary on Lao-tse*. Ascona, Switz.: Artibus Asiae, 1958.

Feuerstein, G. A. *The Essence of Yoga: A Contribution to the Psychohistory of Indian Civilisation*. London: Rider, 1974.

Filliozat, J. "Taoïsme et Yoga." *Dan Viet Nam* 3 (1949):113–20; and *Journal Asiatique* 257, nos. 1, 2 (1969):41–87.

Giles, Herbert A. *A History of Chinese Literature*. London: William Heinemann, 1901.

————. *The Remains of Lao Tzŭ*. Hong Kong: China Mail, 1886.

Harvard-Yenching Institute. *A Concordance to Chuang Tzu*. Sinological Index Series, Supplement no. 20. Cambridge, Mass.: Harvard University Press, 1956.

Henricks, Robert G. "Character Variants in the Ma-wang-tui Texts of the *Lao-tzu*." *Tsing Hua Journal of Chinese Studies*, n.s. 13, nos. 1, 2 (December 1981):221–84.

————. "Examining the Ma-wang-tui Silk Texts of the *Lao-tzu*: With Special Note of Their Differences from the Wang Pi Text." *T'oung Pao* 65, nos. 4, 5 (1979):166–99.

————. *Lao-Tzu: Te-Tao Ching: A New Translation Based on the Recently Discovered Ma-wang-tui Texts*. New York: Ballantine, 1989.

————. "A Note on the Question of Chapter Divisions in the Ma-wang-tui Manuscripts of the *Lao-tzu*." *Early China* 4 (1978–79):49–51.

————. "On the Chapter Divisions in the *Lao-tzu*." *Bulletin of the School of Oriental and African Studies* 45, no. 3 (1982):501–24.

————. "The Philosophy of Lao-tzu Based on the Ma-wang-tui Texts: Some

Preliminary Observations." *Society for the Study of Chinese Religions Bulletin* 9 (Fall 1981):59–78.

Iyengar, B. K. S. *Light on Yoga: Yoga Dipika.* London: George Allen and Unwin, 1965. Reprint. New York: Shocken, 1975.

Izutsu, Toshihiko. *Sufism and Taoism: A Comparative Study of Key Philosophical Concepts.* Berkeley: University of California Press, 1984.

Kaltenmark, Max. *Lao Tzu and Taoism.* Translated from the French by Roger Greaves. Stanford: Stanford University Press, 1969.

Kuo Mo-jo. "Ku-tai Wen-tzu chih Pien-cheng te Fa-chan [The Development of the Dialectics of Ancient Script]." *K'ao-ku* [Archaeology] 3 (1972):2–13.

Kuvalayananda, Svami. *Prāṇāyāma.* Bombay: Popular Prakashan, 1966.

Lau, D. C., trans. and annot. *Tao Te Ching.* Hong Kong: Chinese University Press, 1982.

Lin, Paul J. *A Translation of Lao Tzu's Tao Te Ching and Wang Pi's Commentary.* Ann Arbor: University of Michigan Center for Chinese Studies, 1977.

Ma Hsü-lun. *Lao Tzu Chiao-ku* [Lao Tzu: Collation and commentary]. Peking: Ku-chi Ch'u-pan-she, 1956.

Mair, Victor H. *T'ang Transformation Texts: A Study of the Buddhist Contribution to the Rise of Vernacular Fiction and Drama in China.* Harvard-Yenching Institute Monograph Series, no. 28. Cambridge, Mass.: Harvard University Council on East Asian Studies, 1989.

————, trans., annot., and intro. *Tun-huang Popular Narratives.* Cambridge: Cambridge University Press, 1983.

*Ma-wang-tui Han Mu Po-shu* (I) [Silk Manuscripts from the Han Tombs at Ma-wang-tui], I. Peking: Wen-wu Ch'u-pan-she, 1974. Includes complete photofacsimiles of the manuscripts.

Miller, Barbara Stoler, trans. *The Bhagavad-Gita: Krishna's Counsel in Time of War.* New York: Columbia University Press and Bantam, 1986.

Needham, Joseph, with the collaboration of Lu Gwei-Djen. *Science and Civ-*

*ilisation in China.* Vol. 5, *Chemistry and Chemical Technology;* Part V, "Spagyrical Discovery and Invention: Physiological Alchemy." Cambridge: Cambridge University Press, 1983.

Pott, P.H. *Yoga and Yantra: Their Interrelation and Their Significance for Indian Archaeology.* Translated from the Dutch by Rodney Needham. Koninklijk Instituut voor Taal-, Land- en Volkenkunde, Translation Series, no. 8. The Hague: Martinus Nijhoff, 1966.

Radhakrishnan, S., ed., trans., and annot. *The Principal Upaniṣads.* London: George Allen and Unwin, 1953.

Ramdas, Swami. *The Pathless Path.* Bombay: Bharatiya Vidya Bhavan, 1964.

Rump, Ariane, in collaboration with Wing-tsit Chan. *Commentary on the Lao Tzu by Wang Pi.* Society for Asian and Comparative Philosophy Monograph no. 6. Honolulu: University of Hawaii Press, 1979.

Sargeant, Winthrop, trans. *The Bhagavad Gītā.* Rev. ed. by Christopher Chapple. Albany: State University of New York Press, 1984.

Schwartz, Benjamin I. *The World of Thought in Ancient China.* Cambridge, Mass.: Belknap (Harvard University Press), 1985.

Seidel, Anna K. "Taoism." Macropaedia of *The New Encyclopaedia Britannica.* Chicago: Encyclopaedia Britannica, 1983. Vol. 17, pp. 1034b–1044b.

Shaughnessy, Edward L. "Historical Perspectives on the Introduction of the Chariot into China." *Harvard Journal of Asiatic Studies* 48, no. 1 (June 1988):189–237.

———. "Western Cultural Innovations in China, 1200 B.C." *Sino-Platonic Papers* 11 (July 1989).

Shima Kunio. *Rōshi Kōsei* [Variorum Edition of the Laozi]. Tokyo: Kyūko Shoin, 1973.

Strickmann, Michel. "History of Taoism" and "Taoist Literature." Macropaedia of *The New Encyclopaedia Britannica.* Chicago: Encyclopaedia Britannica, 1983. Vol. 17, pp. 1044b–1050b and 1051a–1055a.

Vasilyev, L. S. "Dao i Brakhman: Fenomen Iznachal'noi Verkhovnoi Vseobshchnosti." In *Dao i Daosizm v Kitae.* Akademiya Nauk SSSR, Ordena Tru-

dovogo Krasnogo Znameni Institut Vostokovedeniya. Moscow: "Nauka,"
Glavnaya Redaktsiya Vostochnoi Literatur'i, 1982.

Waley, Arthur. *The Way and Its Power: A Study of the Tao Te Ching and Its
Place in Chinese Thought.* New York: Grove, 1958.

Warren, Henry Clarke, trans. *Buddhism in Translations.* Cambridge, Mass.:
Harvard University, 1909.

Watson, Burton, trans. *The Complete Works of Chuang Tzu.* New York: Columbia University Press, 1968.

## About the Translator

VICTOR H. MAIR is one of America's foremost translators of ancient Chinese. He is Professor of Chinese Language and Literature in the Department of Oriental Studies at the University of Pennsylvania in Philadelphia. His many acclaimed publications include *Tun-huang Popular Narratives*, *T'ang Transformation Texts*, and *Painting and Performance: Chinese Picture Recitation and its Indian Genesis*.